Luzena Stanley Wilson
1819–1902
The feminine portion of the population was so small
that I have had men come forty miles over the mountains, just to
look at me, and I never was called a handsome woman, in my
best days, even by my most ardent admirers.
The only known photograph of Luzena, circa 1880,
Mills College Alumnae Association.

MY CHECKERED LIFE

Luzena Stanley Wilson in Early California

by Fern L. Henry

with reprint of

LUZENA STANLEY WILSON: '49er

originally published by
Eucalyptus Press
1937

To Mary,

Fern Henry

December 2006

CARL MAUTZ PUBLISHING
2003

Cover: Frenzeny and Tavernier, *Harper's Weekly*.
Frontispiece: Luzena Stanley Wilson circa 1880, Mills College Alumnae Association.

Cover designed by Carl Mautz
Layout designed by Rosemarie Mossinger

Cataloguing-in-Publication Data:
    Henry, Fern L.
    My Checkered Life: Luzena Stanley Wilson in Early California
    First edition
    1. California—History, 2. California—Gold Rush, 3. Women—California
Includes bibliographical references and index.
Hardcover ISBN: 1-887694-53-6
Softcover ISBN: 1-887694-52-8

Carl Mautz Publishing
15472 Shannon Way
Nevada City CA 95959
Telephone: 530-478-1610
Fax: 530-478-0466
E-mail: cmautz@carlmautz.com
Web Site: http://www.carlmautz.com

CONTENTS

INTRODUCTION
BY GARY F. KURUTZ

THE CALIFORNIA GOLD RUSH produced one of the great bodies of eyewitness literature in American history. Only the journals and letters written during the Civil War exceeded the rush to California in numbers and in life and death drama. Unlike the Civil War, men and women came to this new El Dorado searching for instant riches, rather than fighting for a political and moral cause. Many of these Argonauts possessed remarkable powers of observation and penned scores of diaries and thousands of letters, many of which were preserved by family members, or published as books or as articles in local newspapers.

The earthshaking events of 1849 and the years immediately following produced another important category of Gold Rush literature, the reminiscence. Many participants realized that they had experienced the adventure of a lifetime, even if they did not make a pile, and saw the importance of writing down their recollections of those rambunctious days. Like the contemporary account, many of these were privately printed as a gift for family and friends, or published commercially for a wider audience. As pointed out by Dale L. Morgan in his brilliant bibliographic essay introducing the lengthy reminiscences of Howard C. Gardiner's *In Pursuit of the Golden Dream,* many of the best known accounts fall into this genre. Lewis Manly's *Death Valley in '49,* Peter H. Burnett's *Recollections of an Old Pioneer,* Judge Stephen J. Field's *Reminiscences of Early Days in California,* Dr. Jacob Stillman's *Seeking the Golden Fleece,* Major William Downie's *Hunting for Gold,* and Jessie Benton Frémont's *A Year of American Travel,* to name just a few, all represent superb Gold Rush accounts based on memory. While not as immediate or reliable as the diary or letter, these recollections have added immeasurably to our understanding of California's defining event.

In recent years, with interest in gender studies, and not just the fabled story of the "Boys of '49," accounts by women have been revisited and reexamined with a new perspective and freshness. As has been so often told, women were indeed scarce, but their impact far exceeded their numbers. The letters of Dame Shirley, the observations of Eliza Farnham, the travel account of Dolly Bates, and the recollections of Sarah Royce must be regarded as some of the most memorable descriptions of the Gold Rush. As these ladies proved, not all made a living in gambling and drinking saloons and many, traveling with their families, came as harbingers of civilization and tamers of a barbarous land. They brought stability and helped establish California as a place of permanent residence.

One of those vanguards of civilization was Luzena Stanley Wilson. Arriving in California in 1849 after a long overland journey with her husband, Mason, and two children, she made a lasting mark on her adopted home. Thirty years later, this Forty-niner with the assistance of her daughter, put down her memories of that golden era. These recollections first appeared as a series of articles in *The Argonaut* of San Francisco in 1881 under the simple title of "A Woman's Reminiscences of Early Days" and signed only by the initial "W." In so doing, she presented to the public a rare female perspective about a time period that had already achieved legendary status. Her stirring account of selling a miner a biscuit in exchange for a gold coin and her recall of the queenly status of women in Gold Rush Sacramento are literary nuggets that brought to life a whole era in a manner few others can match. Making a livelihood running a hotel and feeding appreciative and home-sick miners demonstrated the golden opportunity that awaited the gentler sex in that rough and tumble environment. Her modest calico dress, as much as the miner's red shirt, emerges as a potent symbol of the Gold Rush. Because of her extraordinary experiences and eloquence, present day historians and interpreters of those heady days frequently draw upon the recollections of Luzena for their books, articles, speeches, exhibits, films, and websites. In short, she created many quotable quotes and preserved stories worth repeating again and again.

One of the valuable aspects of Luzena Wilson's reminiscences is that she recalled life after the Gold Rush. So many diaries and recollections ended with the arrival in this untamed land and the reader can only surmise what happened to the writer. The Wilsons faced floods, fires, fights, and opportunities won and lost in Sacramento and Nevada City, then moved to the Vaca Valley in Solano County. In their new surroundings, they experienced the waning days of California's rancho economy and culture. But trouble dogged their lives, and as with many pioneer families, the Wilsons struggled, persevered, and struggled again. Luzena recounts the establishment of present day Vacaville, the growth of her family, their education, and the business setbacks of her husband. By itself, Luzena's recollections of early Vacaville, a town based on agriculture and not gold, is an important contribution to the understanding of rural northern California in that volatile decade of the 1850s.

Fern Henry, long an admirer of this gentle but redoubtable Gold Rush lady and an authority on the history of Vacaville and its environs, saw the need to bring out a new edition of this remarkable reminiscence. First published in book form in 1937 by the Eucalyptus Press of Mills College in an attractive edition of only 500 copies, it included an introduction by noted historian and bibliographer Francis P. Farquhar. Long out of print, it is now regarded as a rare book and commands a stiff price in the antiquarian market. Ask any Gold Rush historian to name an important account in need of a being republished, and invariably, Luzena Wilson's *Recollection of Early Days* is on the top of the list. Historians will welcome the return of this narrative and will place it on a shelf full of new editions of Gold Rush classics.

This new edition is much more than a simple reprint or facsimile. Because of the strength of Mrs. Wilson's narrative, it would have been quite easy for Henry to write a new, updated introduction and call it quits. Henry, however, recognized both the strengths and weaknesses of this reminiscent account. While sparkling in its language and packed with dramatic episodes, Mrs. Wilson's narrative, dictated a generation later, cannot help but have a few flaws. The passing of time has a way of confusing and exaggerating events. Drawing upon her considerable research skills, Henry instead chose the much more difficult task of verifying the text, providing context and background, and filling in the blanks. She corrected errors and brought in contemporary narratives of other gold seekers and settlers to support the Wilson text. Because of this approach, she has made an invaluable contribution to the history of the Gold Rush, the role of women in early California, and the story of Vacaville as seen through the experiences of a pioneer family.

Henry took this undertaking one step further, creating an original Wilson family biography by following their trail from its early days in the Quaker environment of North Carolina to life in post-Gold Rush northern California. While Wilson covered a relatively short time period in her reminiscences, Henry tells the whole story by delving into the family background, identifying and tracing her husband's roots and subsequent life after deserting his family, and documenting the fascinating lives of Luzena and her children well into the twentieth century. In short, Henry, through diligent and imaginative historical detective work, presents a remarkable profile of a California family drawn by the familiar notions of health and prosperity in a new land, and in large measure, achieving that elusive goal in spite of life's obstacles. The Wilson family, led and held together by Luzena, represented the bedrock that transformed California from a land of golden dreams to one of realistic opportunity.

GARY F. KURUTZ
California State Library
Sacramento

AUTHOR'S FOREWORD

"There is no need for elaboration," wrote Francis P. Farquhar in the introduction to the original 1937 edition of LUZENA STANLEY WILSON: '49er (see Appendix I, page 204). He maintained that we need no further information on her life before and after the events she described. It takes considerable courage to disagree with such an admirable man as Mr. Farquhar (1887–1974). His resume is weighty: twice the president of the Sierra Club, editor of the Sierra Club Bulletin, author of numerous books and articles on the Sierra Nevada and California history, and a president of both the California Historical Society and the California Academy of Sciences. Mountain climbing was his passion, and in 1989, a mountain peak in the Great Western Divide was named in his honor.

Nonetheless, disagree we must. An oral history, even one as intriguing as Luzena Stanley Wilson's, cannot be taken at face value. One must ask if her memory was accurate and, where possible, seek out other primary sources to confirm her recollections. Fortunately, today's researchers have many tools to use to ferret out such detail, none more powerful than the Internet and the access it provides to libraries, archives and various data bases. A conscientious reader must also consider the possibility that, thirty years after the fact, Mrs. Wilson may have succumbed to the human tendency to recall events selectively. Comparison of her experiences with those of her contemporaries can be a gauge of her objectivity.

Today's reader also needs to know considerably more than Mr. Farquhar thought necessary in 1937, when Eucalyptus Press first published the book. After all, the nineteenth century is more distant now. Mr. Farquhar's life and Mrs. Wilson's life overlapped for a period of fifteen years; the events which shaped her were woven into the fabric of his family as well. However, we need to be reminded of the context. The national debate over slavery, the Civil War, the westward expansion of the United States, the transcontinental railroad—all these profoundly changed our nation. They also directly affected people's lives. By following the Wilsons' stories, we glimpse the personal impact of these larger events, and with this new perspective we are inspired anew to delve deeper into the history of the time.

Furthermore, we are curious to see Luzena's face. Our modern imaginations rely heavily on visual imagery, and photographs, illustrations, personal letters and maps help us forge a meaningful link to the past. The documentary films of Ken Burns and others have shown us the impact of even a single picture accompanied by a first-person narration. The original edition of Mrs. Wilson's reminiscences had fine line drawings by Kathryn Uhl (1910–2000), who was an art instructor at Mills College then. Though excellent in quality, the Uhl drawings lack the evocative power of an actual nineteenth century image. Thus, this reprint of the memoir will include photographs, to add a further dimension to the story.

Finally, recent events have thrust Luzena Stanley Wilson into the spotlight. As interest in women's history has grown, numerous anthologies of women in the western migration have quoted extensively from her book. Readers now have internet access to her memoir through such websites as the Library of Congress, Public Broadcasting System: The West. Luzena was featured at the Oakland Museum as part of their interactive display in celebration of the sesquicentennial of the Gold Rush and California's statehood.

Vacaville, the town that Luzena Wilson and her family helped establish, has also celebrated its 150th anniversary. As the Vacaville community remembers its past, Luzena's story should be brought to the fore and made accessible to the city's present citizens. Like Luzena, I have called Vacaville my home for twenty-eight years and am pleased to offer this book to my hometown as a birthday greeting. I am proud to reintroduce her as a local celebrity. Since Luzena's path also led her through Sacramento, Nevada City and San Francisco, her recollections of the early days there will interest many other readers; and, hopefully, other researchers will reexamine her story.

Luzena's own words provide the framework for this new edition. The newly researched opening chapter tells of Luzena's life back East before the Gold Rush. Then, she begins her own story. Each chapter of her original script appears, followed immediately by a chapter which provides additional information on the events she witnessed. These two threads are woven together until Luzena's narrative ends. Then we trace the rest of her life story, followed by details about the fates of the other Wilson family members. I hope you, the reader, enjoy making Luzena's acquaintance and experience the delight I felt in coming to know this intriguing American family.

FERN L. HENRY
Vacaville, California

FRIENDS' MEETING HOUSE
AT NEW GARDEN NORTH CAROLINA, 1869
ERECTED IN 1791.

DRAWN BY JOHN COLLINS.   COPYRIGHT SECURED

Built in 1791 and large enough to hold more than 1,500 people, the old Meeting House served the New Garden Quaker community for nearly one hundred years. John Collins painted this image of it in 1869. The location is now the site of Guilford College in Greensboro, North Carolina. Friends Historical Collection, Guilford College.

I N 1849, LUZENA STANLEY WILSON JOINED THE CALIFORNIA GOLD RUSH, crossing the continent with her husband and children. Many years later she told the stories of her early pioneer days to her daughter who wrote them down and preserved them. Since Mrs. Wilson was sharing personal recollections with a family member, she omitted many details that were well known to both. No mention was made of how Luzena met her husband or of their lives before 1849; indeed, Mason Wilson appears in many of her anecdotes, yet she never calls him by name. Her vivid stories naturally arouse curiosity and a desire to know more about her. Was her memory accurate? What happened to her in later years?. Tracing her path from her Southern roots, following her migration west, checking the veracity of her stories and learning her eventual fate will complete the portrait of a fascinating frontier woman. Now, one hundred years after her death, both the end and the beginning of her story can be told.

Her family lived in the Piedmont region of North Carolina in a Quaker community established in the 1750s near present-day Greensboro. Her birth is carefully noted in the records of the Quakers who met for worship at the New Garden Monthly Meeting: Luzena Stanley Hunt, May 1, 1819. She was the third daughter born to Asa and Diana Hunt, but only one sister, two-year-old Lydia, was there to welcome her. Rebecca, the firstborn child, died before the age of two. After Luzena, six more children, four girls and two boys, joined the Hunt family according to the available Quaker records.[1]

The youngest son William passed along some Hunt family history to his children who published it as a tribute to him:

> *The family represented by William Gaston Hunt was of southern blood, and his father, Asa Hunt, the descendant of English ancestry. His mother, formerly Diana*

Stanley, was of Quaker birth, in which faith she reared her large family of eight daugh-
ters and two sons, of whom William Gaston Hunt was the youngest, his birth occurring
in Guilford County, North Carolina, February 12, 1827. The means of the family
were rather limited and no large income was derived from the father's work in the milling
business (both lumber and woolen mills) and the conduct of a cotton gin, and through the
early death of his parents, the mother in 1846 and the father two years later, William
G. Hunt found the greater part of his sisters' support upon his shoulders.[2]

Fortunately for historians, the Quakers were instructed by their founder, George Fox, to keep careful records on the Society of Friends, including vital statistics as well as committee work and group decisions. The Hunt family is included in the archives of the New Garden Meeting, and the picture that emerges is more complex and hence, more interesting than the simple portrait that William outlined above.

The first hint of controversy occurred when Asa Hunt and Diana Stanley married. The minutes dated November 27, 1813 state: "A committee was appointed to meet with Asa Hunt regarding his marriage contrary to discipline."[3] A later entry on the same day said: "The Committee reported no satisfaction and disowned Asa Hunt." The young couple failed to follow proper procedure. They were expected to first declare their intentions to the men and women's meetings respectively. Committees would then investigate to see that each was "clear" to marry, meaning not already engaged or already married. Once cleared—a process that might take three months—the couple stood in front of the meet-ing and married one another by exchanging simple vows. The bride was never given away by her father, nor did she ever promise to obey her husband; equal-ity of the sexes was a long-standing Quaker belief; marriage was seen as a partnership. But Asa and Diana did not wait for the investigation phase and apparently they married without telling anyone.

The women's meeting lodged a complaint against Diana in January 1814, "for accomplishing her marriage contrary to discipline." The women who met with Diana found her repentant on February 26, 1814:

The friends appointed last meeting to visit with Diana Hunt report they have attend-
ed thereto with a degree of satisfaction and she appeared at the meeting and offered a
paper condemning her outgoings in marriage which was acceptable.

Later in the year Asa expressed a desire to rejoin the meeting, and finally in January 1815 his request was granted. Back in unity with the Quaker Meeting, the Hunt family took its place in the community.

To educate the children, some Quaker families pooled resources and hired a tutor, but teachers were scarce and public schools even rarer. Most children at that time were educated at home, learning to read and write at the family hearth in the evenings. The Hunt children probably worked alongside their parents in the home and the family business, incorporating their limited book knowledge into practical experience. A small brick schoolhouse was built behind the New Garden Meeting House in 1816, but no records survive to show if the Hunt children ever attended there. The Quakers valued books, especially those concerning science, mathematics and mechanical arts; they shunned music and literature as frivolous pursuits. The community wanted children to grow as sober, useful and faithful citizens.

The social and spiritual center of life was the meeting house where everyone gathered on First Day, their term for Sunday. By tradition, Quakers kept silent in worship, each one attending to the "Inner Light" and trying to respond directly to God. Those who spoke were guided by a clear prompting from this inner voice. The freedom to follow one's own conscience in thought, however, was always balanced by the stern demands of Quaker discipline. The members' behavior, business practices, and personal ethics were under constant peer scrutiny. Complaints could be brought against any member who was seen to be in error. Despite being a freedom-loving people, the Friends placed a high value on conformity and not everyone lived up to the group's standards.

When a Quaker behaved "contrary to discipline," members would visit and earnestly try to persuade him or her of the error. The goal was to have all members of one mind. It was quite easy to run afoul of the rules. For example, members were warned against dancing to a fiddler, using alcohol to excess, charging too much interest on a loan, sleeping in meeting, or worse—not attending at all. A Quaker could be expelled for fighting in a war or battle, owning slaves, or failing to pay debts. This method of discipline involved the Friends intimately in each others' lives. The warmth and support of the community, once lost, could usually be regained by sincere apologies and restitution when appropriate. Since discipline was exercised over the smallest details of everyday life, some members grew restive and penalties became harsher.

The Hunts were among the rebels. Asa Hunt was disowned in 1830 for "having spiritous liquors distilled and taking an oath in Court as a juror." The Women's minutes of January 30, 1836 reveal that Diana and two daughters were defiant when confronted about their behavior: "The preparative meeting complains of Diana Hunt and her Daughters Lydia and Luzena for not attending meeting and deviating from plainness." Plain dress was required of men and women. Ribbons, ruffles or bright colors were forbidden. Even the choice of hat and hair styles were noticed, as were the size of lapels. A month later on February 27, 1836:

> *The friends appointed last month to visit with Diana Hunt and her Daughters Lydia and Luzena report they have had opportunity with Diana and Luzena but they did not appear to be in a disposition to make satisfaction and informed them that Lydia was of the same mind. Therefore, this meeting thinks it best to disown them from being members thereof.*

This is the last mention of the Hunts in the New Garden minutes, so it appears they did not seek reinstatement.

Asa worked as a miller, a practical occupation in the agriculture-based economy of the day. Water mills were common along the many streams and rivers in the area. The Hunt's sawmill converted logs to lumber for construction and their woolen mill and cotton gin served the community's need for fiber, cloth and rope. The Piedmont area was also rich in wildlife with plentiful forests and a congenial climate. Some of the land had been cleared by the native Indians who grew large fields of corn. But survival required hard work even in such a favorable environment. Farming, caring for animals, building houses and barns, weaving cloth, cooking meals and repairing equipment all required human hands. Having taken a principled stand against slavery as a Quaker, Asa would have had to pay wages to all employees at his mills, if indeed he could find anyone to hire. Manual labor was scorned and seen as suitable only for slaves. Thus, on their farms and in their mills, shops and inns, Quakers had a higher overhead and lower profits than their slave-owning competitors. In the North many Quakers grew wealthy, but in the South, relative poverty was a direct consequence of their refusal to own slaves or profit from slave labor.

North Carolina Quakers had been slow to condemn the owning of slaves, although they were taught to "walk cheerfully over the world, answering to that of God in every man."[4] They readily perceived that this admonition included the native American Indians whom they treated with respect. Some Quakers owned slaves, nonetheless, and it took many years of missionary effort and letters from Friends in the northern states and in England before slave owning was officially condemned in the Southern Quaker discipline. Once convinced, the ubiquitous Quaker committees went into action. Slave-owning Friends were visited and "labored with in love" to bring all into unity; several of Asa Hunt's ancestors were active in this work. As for Luzena's own family, the census of

Asa Hunt Family

Asa Hunt
Born November 4, 1790, New Garden Monthly
Meeting, North Carolina
Died circa 1846, Andrew County, Missouri
Father: William Hunt
Mother: Ann Rayl

Diana Stanley
Born May 24, 1796, New Garden Mm., NC
Died circa 1844, Andrew County, MO
Father: William Stanley
Mother: Rebecca Clemmons

Married
November 27, 1813
New Garden Mm., NC

Children

Rebecca Hunt
Born December 12, 1814, New Garden Mm., NC
Died March 16, 1816, New Garden Mm.

Lydia Hunt
Born February 21, 1817, New Garden Mm., NC

Luzena Stanley Hunt
Born May 1, 1819, New Garden Mm., NC
Died July 11, 1902, San Francisco, CA
Married December 19, 1844, Andrew County, MO
Spouse: Mason Wilson

Martha Dillon Hunt
Born August 29, 1821, New Garden Mm., NC
Died June 5, 1903, Marion, Indiana
Married May 5, 1840, New Garden Mm., NC
Spouse: Daniel Mendenhall

Alvis B. Hunt
Born date unknown, New Garden Mm., NC
Died 1852, California
Married April 18, 1849, Andrew County, MO
Spouse: Melisa Ann Hunt

Eliza Hunt
Born November 15, 1825, New Garden Mm., NC
Died January 12, 1907, Vacaville, CA
Married February 10, 1850, St. Joseph, MO
Spouse: William Jackson Dobbins

William Gaston Hunt
Born February 12, 1827, New Garden Mm., NC
Died February 4, 1899, Oakland, CA
Married: 1853, California
Spouse: Jennie Glass Day

Emily Hunt
Born June 1, 1830, New Garden Mm., NC
Died September 1914, Red Bluff, CA
Married March 28, 1852, Sacramento, CA
Spouse: William Burr Harrison Dodson

Harriet Hunt
Born circa 1832, New Garden Mm., NC

1840 shows two male "free coloreds" living with the Asa Hunt family, indicating that they may have been sheltering some freed slaves or employing them in the family business.

Freed slaves certainly needed protection. In North Carolina it was illegal to free slaves without court consent and this was not easily obtained. Further, slaves could easily be captured and sold to a new master. Some Quakers bought slaves to keep black families together. Clearly, the Friends needed legal counsel. Judge William Gaston, a bright Catholic lawyer and ardent opponent of slavery, devised a strategy for them: the North Carolina Yearly Meeting in which all the state's monthly meetings participated, became the owner of all slaves previously owned by Quakers. In the eyes of the law, these 'Quaker Free Negroes' were not free, but the Quakers treated them as such, paying them for their work and keeping families intact. William Gaston must have been a hero to Asa and Diana Hunt, for they named their youngest son after him.

In the years leading up to the Civil War, the Friends became more outspoken on the evils of slavery, believing that the institution was an evil that had infected society. Many felt that as Christians they could no longer live in the South, and a great westward migration began. The revulsion to slavery provided the push to leave, but the promise of a better life elsewhere served to pull settlers to Ohio, Indiana and points west. The records of the New Garden Meeting confirm that at least one hundred families and some individuals departed—254 people—between the years 1800 and 1860. The result was a serious depletion in their ranks.

The Hunts were not counted in the tally of Quakers who left North Carolina since they had been disowned, but the Quakers were not the only people emigrating. One third of the entire state population left in the period between 1815 and 1850. A noted historian who studied the 1850 census concluded, "North Carolina's indifference to education, neglect of resources, resistance to taxation for any purpose, and general backwardness had driven away 405,101 people, two-thirds of whom were white."[5] Poverty and a stagnant economy took their toll; the Hunts were among the many families who decided to seek a better life elsewhere.

For Asa and Diana Hunt, migration was part of a family tradition. Their Quaker forebears had been on the move since the seventeenth century in England. The Society of Friends was formed there in 1644 by George Fox and members were immediately persecuted. Their beliefs were antithetical to the prevailing doctrines of the Anglican Church; the Quakers would not accept the authority of the Church hierarchy, believing that God spoke directly to each person. Twelve years later, two Quaker women landed in Boston, setting off a series of migrations to the new world that was unstoppable, even in the face of virulent Puritan opposition to their coming. The ancestors of both Asa and Diana Hunt emigrated from England. Diana's Stanley ancestors trace their roots to Thomas Stanley who appeared in Virginia around 1690; his origins in England remain open to research. Luzena's great-grandmother Elizabeth (Walker) Stanley could trace her line of descent to the Scottish Stewart kings.[6] Luzena's pride in her Stanley heritage may have been the reason she always used her full name and passed the Stanley name along to her firstborn son, Thomas Stanley Wilson.

By 1843 Asa and Diana Hunt had traveled west with their family to Andrew County, Missouri, and settled on government land just north of St. Joseph, according to William Hunt's account. Under the terms of the Preemptive Act of 1841, settlers were allowed to claim land that had not yet been formally surveyed and offered for sale. They could stake out 160 acres and purchase it from the government before any public sales. In return, the pioneers had to occupy the land for a little over a year, erect some type of building (with at least one window in it!) and begin to clear the land. The prices started at around $1.25 per acre. Asa Hunt may have taken advantage of this opportunity or purchased land at a government auction. After Diana's death in 1846 and Asa's in 1848, the land was claimed by their surviving children. No land records in Asa Hunt's name have been found yet, but his eldest son Alvis B. Hunt owned forty acres in that county as of November 1848.

Asa and Diana Hunt lived to see their daughter Luzena marry at age twenty-five, on December 19, 1844. She wed Mason Wilson in Andrew County, Missouri. Little is known of Mason's early life. He was born in Kentucky and his probable birth date was October 3, 1806. Unconfirmed records indicate his parents were Joseph Thornton Wilson and Elizabeth Grace Fyffe who were married in Mason County, Kentucky in 1799. The first thirty-eight years of Mason's life remain a mystery. Somehow he traveled west where he met Luzena, and the newlyweds made their home in a log cabin on the prairie in Andrew County. Most likely Mason was a farmer, although no evidence has been found to confirm that assumption. Their first son Thomas was born in September 1845, and another son, Jay Crittenden Wilson, arrived in June 1848. Mason and Luzena bought land and had lived on it for just two years when the rumors of gold caught their imagination. Luzena said they abandoned their land and cabin to "the next comer" in their haste to leave. The other Hunt siblings were more cautious, according to brother William's story:

At the time of his parents' demise . . . Three payments had been made upon this land, when, in 1849, at the time of the great gold excitement in the remote lands of California, the Hunts decided to immigrate to the Pacific Coast. After making arrangements to cross the plains in a train of five wagons organized in their home neighborhood, they left with the justice of the peace in the vicinity money with which to make the fourth payment on their land which they desired to retain, as they might wish to return to Missouri and in any event it would give them back their payments by sale. They left their home in Missouri on the first of May, 1849, and were four months en route to Hangtown [Placerville], California. Two months after their arrival there they received a letter from Missouri informing them the justice of the peace was dead and they had forfeited the right to the land as the fourth payment had not been made. This probably influenced their decision to remain permanently in California, for certain it is they never returned to the middle west.[7]

Luzena never went back either. Her own words convey her feelings that spring morning in 1849 as she and her family set off on their great adventure.

Pen and ink sketch depicts a cabin of the mid-1800s, such as the one left behind by Luzena and her husband. Private collection.

NOTES

1. William Wade Hinshaw, *Encyclopedia of Quaker Genealogy*, 502. The ancestry records of the Latter Day Saints Church list these six additional children; the original source cited (Swarthmore College collection of Quaker records) did not contain the data. The genealogical data on the Hunt siblings cited is the best information available, but is not confirmed.

2. Professor J. M. Guinn, A.M., *History of the State of California and Biographical Record of the Sacramento Valley*, 449.

3. Minutes of the New Garden Monthly Meeting, Friends Historical Collection. All subsequent quotes from the New Garden minutes are from the same source.

4. Hiram H. Hilty, *New Garden Friends Meeting*, 26.

5. William S. Powell, *North Carolina Through Four Centuries*, 250.

6. Alvin L. Anderson, Ph.D., *Stanley and Allied Families: Descendants of the Quaker Stanley Families of Colonial Virginia*, Volume Two, 3, 9–10.

7. Guinn, 449.

AUTHOR'S NOTE

Kathryn Uhl's original drawings are reproduced at the beginning of each of Luzena's chapters as they appeared in the 1937 volume.

2

Luzena: ON THE OVERLAND TRAIL

Early Summer 1849

THE GOLD EXCITEMENT SPREAD LIKE WILDFIRE, even out to our log cabin in the prairie, and as we had almost nothing to lose, and we might gain a fortune, we early caught the fever. My husband grew enthusiastic and wanted to start immediately, but I would not be left behind. I thought where he could go I could, and where I went I could take my two little toddling babies. Mother-like, my first thought was of my children. I little realized then the task I had undertaken. If I had, I think I should still be in my log cabin in Missouri. But when we talked it all over, it sounded like such a small task to go out to California, and once there fortune, of course, would come to us.

It was the work of but a few days to collect our forces for the march into the new country, and we never gave a thought to selling our section, but left it, with two years' labor, for the next comer. Monday we were to be off. Saturday we looked over our belongings, and threw aside what was not absolutely necessary. Beds we must have, and something to eat. It was a strange but comprehensive load which we stowed away in our "prairie-schooner," and some things which I thought necessities when we started became burdensome luxuries, and before many days I dropped by the road-side a good many unnecessary pots and kettles, for on bacon and flour one can ring but few changes, and it requires but few vessels to cook them. One luxury we had which other emigrants nearly always lacked—fresh milk. From our gentle "mulley" cow I never parted. She followed our train across the desert, shared our food and water, and our fortunes, good or ill, and lived in California to a serene old age, in a paradise of green clover and golden stubble-fields, full to the last of good works.

Well, on that Monday morning, bright and early, we were off. With the first streak of daylight my last cup of coffee boiled in the wide fire-place, and the sun was scarcely above the horizon when we were on the road to California. The first day's slow jogging brought us to the Missouri River, over which we were ferried in the twilight, and our first camp fire was lighted in Indian Territory, which spread in one unbroken, unnamed waste from the Missouri River to the border line of California. Here commenced my terrors. Around us in every direction were groups of Indians sitting, standing, and on horseback, as many as two hundred in the camp. I had read and heard whole volumes of their bloody deeds, the massacre of harmless white men, torturing helpless women, carrying away captive innocent babes. I felt my children the most precious in the wide world, and I lived in an agony of dread that first night. The Indians were friendly, of course, and swapped ponies for whisky and tobacco with the gathering bands of emigrants, but I, in the most tragi-comic manner, sheltered my babies with my own body, and felt imaginary arrows pierce my flesh a hundred times during the night. At last the morning broke, and we were off. I strained my eyes with watching, held my breath in suspense, and all day long listened for the whiz of bullets or arrows. The second night out we were still surrounded by Indians, and I begged my husband to ask at a neighboring camp if we might join with them for protection. It was the camp of the "Independence Co.," with five mule-teams, good wagons, banners flying, and a brass band playing. They sent back word they "didn't want to be troubled with women and children; they were going to California." My anger at their insulting answer roused my courage, and my last fear of Indians died a sudden death. "I am only a woman," I said, "but I am going to California, too, and without the help of the Independence Co.!" With their lively mules they soon left our slow oxen far behind, and we lost sight of them. The first part of the trip was over a monotonous level. Our train consisted only of six wagons, but we were never alone. Ahead, as far as the eye could reach, a thin cloud of dust marked the route of the trains, and behind us, like the trail of a great serpent, it extended to the edge of civilization. The travelers were almost all men, but a mutual aim and a chivalric spirit in every heart raised up around me a host of friends, and not a man in the camp but would have screened me with his life from insult or injury. I wonder if in the young men around us a woman could find the same unvarying courtesy and kindness, the same devotion and honest, manly friendship that followed me in the long trip across the plains, and my checkered life in the early days of California!

The traveler who flies across the continent in palace cars, skirting occasionally the old emigrant road, may think that he realizes the trials of such a journey. Nothing but actual experience will give one an idea of the plodding, unvarying monotony, the vexations, the exhaustive energy, the throbs of hope, the depths of despair, through which we lived. Day after day, week after week, we went through the same weary routine of breaking camp at daybreak, yoking the oxen, cooking our meagre rations over a fire of sage-brush and scrub-oak; packing up again, coffee-pot and camp-kettle; washing our scanty wardrobe in the little streams we crossed; striking camp again at sunset, or later if wood and water were scarce. Tired, dusty, tried in temper, worn out in patience, we had to go over the weary experience tomorrow. No excitement, but a broken-down wagon, or the extra preparation made to cross a river, marked our way for many miles. The Platte was the first great water-course we crossed. It is a peculiar, wide, shallow stream, with a quicksand bed. With the wagon-bed on blocks twelve or fourteen inches thick to raise it out of the water, some of the men astride of the oxen, some of them wading waist-deep, and all goading the poor beasts to keep them moving, we started across. The water poured into the wagon in spite of our precautions and floated off some of our few movables; but we landed safely on the other side, and turned to see the team behind us stop in mid-stream. The frantic driver shouted, whipped, belabored the stubborn animals in vain, and the treacherous sand gave way under their feet. They sank slowly, gradually, but surely. They went out of sight inch by inch, and the water rose over the moaning beasts. Without a struggle they disappeared beneath the surface. In a little while the broad South Platte swept on its way, sunny, sparkling, placid, without a ripple to mark where a lonely man parted with all his fortune.

In strange contrast was the North Platte which we next crossed, a boiling, seething, turbulent stream, which foamed and whirled as if enraged at the imprisoning banks. Two days we spent at its edge, devising ways and means. Finally huge sycamore trees were felled and pinned with wooden pins into the semblance of a raft, on which we were floated across where an eddy in the current touched the opposite banks. And so, all the way, it was a road strewn with perils, over a strange, wild country. Sometimes over wide prairies, grass-grown, and deserted save by the startled herds of buffalo and elk; sometimes through deep, wild cañons, where the mosses were like a carpet beneath our feet, and the overhanging trees shut out the sunshine for days together; sometimes over high mountains, where at every turn a new road had to be cleared, we always carried with us tired bodies and often discouraged hearts. We frequently met men who had given up the struggle, who had lost their teams, abandoned their wagons, and, with their blankets on their back, were tramping home.

Everything was at first weird and strange in those days, but custom made us regard the most unnatural events as usual. I remember even yet with a shiver the first time I saw a man buried without the formality of a funeral and the ceremony of coffining. We were sitting by the camp fire, eating breakfast, when I saw two men digging and watched them with interest, never dreaming their melancholy object until I saw them bear from their tent the body of their comrade, wrapped in a soiled gray blanket, and lay it on the ground. Ten minutes later the soil was filled in, and in a short half hour the caravan moved on, leaving the lonely stranger asleep in the silent wilderness, with only the winds, the owls, and coyotes to chant a dirge. Many an unmarked grave lies by the old emigrant road, for hard work and privation made wild ravages in the ranks of the pioneers, and brave souls gave up the battle and lie there forgotten, with not even a stone to note the spot where they sleep the unbroken, dreamless sleep of death. There was no time then to wait, no time to mourn over friend or kindred, no time for anything but the ceaseless march for gold.

There was not time to note the great natural wonders that lay along the route. Some one would speak of a remarkable valley, a group of cathedral-like rocks, some mineral springs, a salt basin, but we never deviated from the direct route to see them. Once as we halted near the summit of the Rocky Mountains for our "nooning," digging through three or four inches of soil we found a stratum of firm, clear ice, six or eight inches in thickness, covering the whole level space for several acres where our train had stopped. I do not think even yet I have ever heard a theory accounting for the strange sheet of ice lying hard and frozen in mid-summer three inches below the surface.

After a time the hard traveling and worse roads told on our failing oxen, and one day my husband said to me, "Unless we can lighten the wagon we shall be obliged to drop out of the train, for the oxen are about to give out." So we looked over our load, and the only things we found we could do without were three sides of bacon and a very dirty calico apron which we laid out by the roadside. We remained all day in camp, and in the meantime I discovered my stock of lard was out. Without telling my husband, who was hard at work mending the wagon, I cut up the bacon, tried out the grease, and had my lard can full again. The apron I looked at twice and thought it would be of some use yet if clean, and with the aid of the Indian soap-root, growing around the camp, it became quite a respectable addition to my scanty wardrobe. The next day the teams, refreshed by the whole day's rest and good grazing, seemed as well as ever, and my husband told me several times what a "good thing it was we left those things; that the oxen seemed to travel as well again."

Long after we laughed over the remembrance of that day, and his belief that the absence of the three pieces of bacon and the dirty apron could work such a change.

A pioneer family with young children and a milk cow, partially visible at far left, was depicted in an engraving by Frenzeny and Tavernier and published by Harper's Weekly. *Private collection.*

3

It was a road strewn with perils . . .

LUZENA AND HER FAMILY WERE AMONG THE MORE THAN 25,000 people who walked west that year. Her account of the overland journey covers many of the topics common to Gold Rush memoirs, of which there are hundreds. This massive migration was the dramatic event of the time and remains the subject of romance and folklore today. While acknowledging that the experience could not be adequately described in words, the forty-niners were well aware that they were living through a signature event and they wanted to preserve their stories. Since Luzena told her story privately, she never gave the names of her traveling companions in the other wagons, beyond noting that they were all from the same area.

It is quite possible that Luzena's brothers and sisters were in the same wagon train as the Wilson family. Her brother William Hunt said he left with his siblings, but he also omitted their names. A few Hunt sisters definitely can be eliminated from the list. Martha Hunt had married around 1840 and settled in Indiana with her family. Eliza remained in Missouri where she married Dr. William Dobbins early in 1850; they came to California later that year. Lydia Hunt has not been traced thus far, but all the other Hunt siblings were forty-niners. The older brother Alvis Hunt married his bride Melissa Ann just two weeks before setting off on the trail, which certainly provided them a honeymoon to remember. Emily and Harriet, the two youngest siblings, were probably along as well, since they show up in the early census of California.

The five Hunts and the four Wilsons probably traveled together, since they had lived near each other in Missouri and left at the same time. Granted, there are discrepancies; Luzena remembers a wagon train of six and William's count was five. William is precise about the departure date of May 1, 1849 which was a Tuesday and coincidentally, Luzena's thirtieth birthday; Luzena said only that it was a Monday morning. Perhaps the Wilsons lived some miles apart from the Hunt siblings and they met along the way. None of the wagon train lists or overland registries record their names. But a newspaper in St. Joseph, Missouri April 27, stated that the the Independent Company from Illinois was planning to leave in two days.[1] Perhaps this was the Independence Company Luzena encountered on her second night out on the trail. St. Joseph was the likely point of departure for the Wilsons and the Hunts, since it was only a few miles south of Andrew County. Luzena said they reached the Missouri River and crossed it on their first day of travel.

As Luzena noted, most of the immigrants were men, but one authoritative researcher estimated that women made up as much as ten percent of the wagon train population in 1849. According to a notable study of Gold Rush women, "Even in 1849 when the most impetuous rushed west first, nearly every trail diary records the presence of families—wives, mother, sister, and daughters."[2] Since wagons passed one another frequently on the trail, Luzena undoubtedly had contact with other women in addition to the sisters who may have been in her own wagon company.

The Wilson's wagon, like most, was overloaded at the beginning. As the long journey took its toll on the oxen and pioneers, many belongings were abandoned. These excess goods were scavenged by Indians or enterprising merchants who later sold the stuff to outfit other wagon trains. Most wagons were pulled by oxen, although mules were sometimes used. Luzena did not say how many yoke of oxen her family had, but two to four pairs of the beasts were common. Sometimes cows were also yoked and made to pull as well, but such a workload would eventually dry up the milk supply. Luzena dearly loved her "mulley cow," a pet name for a cow that indicated the animal was hornless. Milk was needed for her two growing boys, Thomas age 3½, and Jay age 1, and this particular cow probably trudged along behind the wagon. If there was extra milk in the morning, it might have been hung up in the wagon for the day's march. By evening, the continuous jolting of the wagon would have produced butter and buttermilk for supper.

A cow was indeed a luxury, for the cuisine on the trail was spartan. Luzena remembered the "meagre rations" consisting mainly of two ingredients: bacon and flour which she cooked over an open campfire. George Thissell, an Ohio carriage-maker who would eventually become a neighbor of Luzena's in California, described the daily menu in his outfit which started west the same year:

> *If bread was to be made, a large tin pan was used as a kneading-trough. A liberal quantity of saleratus [baking soda] and warm water were stirred together; the requisite*

amount of flour and salt were added, and the dough well kneaded. The dough was flattened out until about one inch thick; then it was placed in an old-fashioned skillet or dutch oven with an iron lid. It was then set on the coals, and a small fire was built on the lid, and by the time the meat was fried and the coffee made, the bread would be done. Sometimes the top and bottom would be burned as black as a coal, while the center was still raw.[3]

No doubt Luzena's recipe was similar, though perhaps her technique was more refined. The usual meat was bacon as Luzena recalled, although skillful hunters

OVERLAND TRAIL

The Overland Trail presented the emigrants with various alternate routes in their 2,200-mile journey from Missouri to California. Luzena did not specify the exact path of the Wilson's wagon train after it passed over the Continental Divide. The majority of wagons in early 1849 took Sublette's Cutoff, but after Hudspeth's Cutoff was established in mid-July, it became the favored choice. Since she never mentioned Salt Lake City, her group probably bypassed that settlement. Map from They Saw the Elephant, *Jo Ann Levy.*

William James Pleasants published his Forty-niner memoir in 1906, dedicating it to his "noble father." Pleasants Valley, lying between the towns of Vacaville and Winters, was named for this pioneer family. William eventually owned 2,000 acres in the valley where he raised orchard and grain crops, livestock, and brought up his nine children. He died in 1919 at age 84. Fairfield Public Library.

could also supply fresh meat. Deer, antelope, fish and grouse were eaten when available. William Pleasants, another neighbor-to-be of theWilsons, noted:

> *Camp was always well supplied with fresh buffalo hump, antelope steak, and now and then for a change buffalo marrow would be served. . . .These were great times for the younger sportsmen. The duties of driving wagons every other day devolved upon them, but their leisure moments were spent in the chase, and their share in the exciting sport was by no means limited.*[4]

Wagons could travel about fifteen miles a day when the going was smooth, but progress slowed considerably in rough terrain. Finding a campsite with grazing each night was a major task; as the summer advanced, grass and water became scarce. The trail was crowded with wagon trains visible to one another, and as Luzena said, "we were never alone." All were competing for the same resources:

firewood, fresh water and food for the livestock. The animals were often driven miles off the trail to graze, herded back at daybreak, and yoked up again. If the oxen were frightened into a stampede, more valuable time was lost in rounding them up.

The daily routine was exhausting and monotonous to Luzena; she said she took no side trips for sightseeing. Her workload was heavy, since she had to care for two lively children in addition to the numerous chores she mentioned. But fifteen-year-old William Pleasants who was traveling with his father and brother had time to climb Independence Rock and sign his name. As one of the junior members of a large wagon train, he had more leisure and energy for pursuit of pleasure. According to others, there were opportunities for socializing. George Thissell wrote:

> *Those trains that passed and repassed each other were known all the way across the plains, and often visited each other at night and had a dance, for in nearly every train there was a violin. The most pleasant part of the trip across the plains in '49–'50 was around the camp-fire. Supper over, dishes and pots out of the way, we would gather around the camp-fire and relate the scenes of the day, and spin long yarns. Some played the violin, others the accordeon. A few would play cards, while the young men would sing their favorite California songs. . . . 'O Susanna, Don't you cry for me, I'm going to California, Some gold dust for to see.'*

Luzena recollected none of these musical evenings nor any other social highlights. Apart from the humorous story about Mason's lightening the load on the oxen by supposedly jettisoning some bacon and an apron, her stories of the trail are markedly serious in tone. But other travelers found romance, according to Thissell. Isaac (Ike) Decker and Lavinia Pond, who would also become Luzena's California neighbors, actually met and married along the emigrant trail:

> *On the bank of the creek, beneath a canopy of willows and wild grapes vines, the ceremony took place that made the twain one flesh. J. M. Robinson, justice of the peace, in a short, simple service, pronounced the young pioneers man and wife. . . .The old, greasy wagon sheets were spread on the ground for tablecloths and the wedding dinner was served upon them. . . . Gathered around the wagon sheets were over forty guests, members of the newly-wedded couple's own train, seated on the ground, while the bride and groom sat at the head of the table, on an ox yoke. Pots and dishes out of the way, the dance commenced, and lasted till the small hours of the morning. Next morning six big Indians came to the camp. Ike looked savage, reached for his gun, and got between the Indians and his bride. A strange sensation tingled all over her at that moment, and she shuddered*

as if with sudden cold. The chief soon dispelled her fears, for in broken English he congratulated them on their big war-dance. The truth is, every Indian for five miles around had heard the racket, and could think of nothing but a war-dance. It struck terror to the redskins, and they troubled the train no more.

The fear of Indians was paramount for many pioneers, at least at the outset of the journey. These early terrors were often laid to rest, as Luzena's were, after friendly encounters. William Pleasants recalled:

In passing through that section of country that is now the State of Kansas, we met with a great many Indians belonging to different tribes, but they were invariably friendly and gave us no trouble. In fact, more than once we found them valuable allies when it became necessary to cross some of the larger streams. Our stock could be made to swim to the other side, but the wagons must be ferried over. So, procuring from our savage friends about eight canoes, we would lash them firmly together, side by side, and then across the whole lay strong poles about one foot apart. These were fastened securely to the canoes with inch-wide buffalo thongs, and with this hastily improvised structure the wagons would be safely ferried across the widest and most turbulent streams.

Sometimes, though, Indians stole, begged, or tried to extort tolls from the settlers, and there were instances where they attacked, killing or kidnaping the pioneers. As the years went by and immigrant numbers grew, hostilities increased.

William Pleasants had one dangerous encounter with Indians, but it happened on his second trip across the continent in 1856 when he was escorting his youngest brother and three sisters to California. In the skirmish, a deflected bullet struck Harvey, the brother, in the groin; Harvey survived the attack but the bullet was still in his body when he died more than a decade later. In later years, William wrote:

I began to understand and appreciate the extreme bitterness with which the Indian regarded the encroachments of the whites, realizing, as he no doubt did, that no matter in what manner or how long he might resist, the superior intelligence of his foe must in the end conquer. Forced further and further back, away from the beloved lands where the bones of his fathers moldered, he could see that it was only a question of time when his proud race would be doomed to extinction. The wild game that now nourished him and his loved ones must soon disappear before the numberless rifles of his masters. Want, physical decay and disease must follow, and in the end a race of men worthy of a better fate will have perished from the face of the earth and not one left to tell of the tragedy. Ah, well, 'tis the old, old story being repeated, and that has been repeated over and over again, since the world first began, the survival of the fittest, and man's inhumanity to man.

Disease and accidents claimed more victims among the immigrants than Indian attacks. William Pleasants chronicled the name of each man in his company who died of cholera and wrote movingly of the spot where each burial took place. Likewise, Thissell mourned the loss of a friend:

> *Though there were many pleasant times and happy hours in camp, there were times when every heart was filled with sorrow. July 20 had been a long and weary day. . . . Uncle Tobin, as he was called by all, lay suffering in his tent. . . . I could hear him offer up his feeble prayer and in low accents sing his favorite song: 'On the other side of Jordan, In the sweet fields of Eden, Where the tree of Life is blooming, There is rest for me.' Poor old soul, that was his last song on earth. . . . We gathered wild flowers and strewed them on his grave, for we had all learned to love Uncle Tobin.*

Cholera claimed many travelers and the dead were often buried hurriedly. Luzena was shocked by the quick roadside burial she witnessed, and for good reason; bodies laid to rest

George Washington Thissell (1829–1908) started west in 1849, but illness forced a nine-month stopover in Iowa, and he arrived in California in 1850. He soon returned east to marry, and eventually moved to Solano County where he made a home for his wife, Asberrene, and six children. His 1903 book features his own experiences on the overland trail, as well as stories he gathered from friends and neighbors. Dietz Collection, Vacaville Museum.

The rigors of the overland trek are evident in this engraving from J. W. Buel's Metropolitan Life Unveiled. *California State Library.*

in shallow graves with no protective coffin were often dug up by coyotes or wolves. She did not mention any deaths in her own wagon train, but she may have heard the stories of dying people being abandoned to a lonely fate as their companions hurried on to the gold fields.

In spite of the sorrows and toil, the beauty and variety of nature's wonders continued to impress the immigrants. Even Luzena admitted that in the Rocky Mountains she took time to dig down and discover ice beneath her feet on a summer day at famous Ice Slough. In the Blue Canyon of these same Rockies, George Thissell paused to admire "the grandest and most enchanting scenery we had yet beheld." Nearby was a mountain of a different sort.

As I stood beside great piles of bacon and flour, piled higher than my head, a notice on every pile, 'This is clean; help yourself,' little did I dream that, long before we reached the gold fields, many of us would be starving to death. Here in one pile was more than five tons of flour and bacon, left behind to lighten up the loads. This the Indians would not eat for fear of poison.

By the time Luzena reached the desert, many travelers were abandoning other possessions as well as their wagons and animals, proceeding on foot to save themselves.

NOTES

1.   Louis J. Rasmussen, *California Wagon Train Lists,* Volume One, 43.
2.   Jo Ann Levy, *They Saw the Elephant,* xvi–xvii.
3.   G. W. Thissell, *Crossing the Plains in '49,* 84.
4.   William J. Pleasants, *Twice Across the Plains: 1849 and 1856,* 18.

Luzena: THE FORTY-MILE DESERT
1849

Our long tramp had extended over three months when we entered the desert, the most formidable of all the difficulties we had encountered. It was a forced march over the alkali plain, lasting three days, and we carried with us the water that had to last, for both men and animals, till we reached the other side. The hot earth scorched our feet; the grayish dust hung about us like a cloud, making our eyes red, and tongues parched, and our thousand bruises and scratches smart like burns. The road was lined with the skeletons of the poor beasts who had died in the struggle. Sometimes we found the bones of men bleaching beside their broken-down and abandoned wagons. The buzzards and coyotes, driven away by our presence from their horrible feasting, hovered just out of reach. The night that we camped in the desert my husband came to me with the story of the "Independence Company." They, like hundreds of others had given out on the desert; their mules gone, many of their number dead, the party broken up, some gone back to Missouri, two of the leaders were here, not distant forty yards, dying of thirst and hunger. Who could leave a human creature to perish in this desolation? I took food and water and found them bootless, hatless, ragged and tattered, moaning in the starlight for death to relieve them from torture. They called me an angel; they showered blessings on me; and when they recollected that they had refused me their protection that day on the Missouri, they dropped on their knees there in the sand and begged my forgiveness. Years after, they came to me in my quiet home in a sunny valley in California, and the tears streamed down their bronzed and weather-beaten cheeks as they thanked me over and over again for my small kindness. Gratitude was not so rare a quality in those days as now.

It was a hard march over the desert. The men were tired out goading on the poor oxen which seemed ready to drop at every step. They were covered with a thick coating of dust, even to the red tongues which hung from their mouths swollen with thirst and heat. While we were yet five miles from the Carson River, the miserable beasts seemed to scent the freshness in the air, and they raised their heads and traveled briskly. When only a half mile of distance intervened, every animal seemed spurred by an invisible imp. They broke into a run, a perfect stampede, and refused to be stopped until they had plunged neck deep in the refreshing flood; and when they were unyoked, they snorted, tossed their heads, and rolled over and over in the water in their dumb delight. It would have been pathetic had it not been so funny, to see those poor, patient, overworked, hard-driven beasts, after a journey of two thousand miles, raise heads and tails and gallop at full speed, an emigrant wagon with flapping sides jolting at their heels. At last we were near our journey's end. We had reached the summit of the Sierra, and had begun the tedious journey down the mountain side. A more cheerful look came to every face; every step lightened; every heart beat with new aspirations. Already we began to forget the trials and hardships of the past, and to look forward with renewed hope to the future. The first man we met was about fifty miles above Sacramento. He had ridden on ahead, bought a fresh horse and some new clothes, and was coming back to meet his train. The sight of his white shirt, the first I had seen for four long months, revived in me the languishing spark of womanly vanity; and when he rode up to the wagon where I was standing, I felt embarrassed, drew down my ragged sun-bonnet over my sunburned face, and shrank from observation. My skirts were worn off in rags above my ankles; my sleeves hung in tatters above my elbows; my hands brown and hard, were gloveless; around my neck was tied a cotton square, torn from a discarded dress; the soles of my leather shoes had long ago parted company with the uppers; and my husband and children and all the camp, were habited like myself, in rags.

A day or two before, this man was one of us; today, he was a messenger from another world, and a stranger, so much influence does clothing have on our feelings and intercourse with our fellow men. It was almost dusk of the last day of September 1849, that we reached the end of our journey in Sacramento.

My poor tired babies were asleep on the mattress in the bottom of the wagon, and I peered out into the gathering gloom, trying to catch a glimpse of our destination. The night before I had cooked my supper on the camp fire, as usual, when a hungry miner, attracted by the unusual sight of a woman, said to me, "I'll give you five dollars, ma'am, for them biscuit." It sounded like a fortune to me, and I looked at him to see if he meant it. And as I hesitated at such, to me, a very remarkable proposition, he repeated his offer to purchase, and said he would give ten dollars for bread made by a woman, and laid the shining gold piece in my hand. I made some more biscuit for my family, told my husband of my good fortune, and put the precious coin away as a nest-egg for the wealth we were to gain. In my dreams that night I saw crowds of bearded miners striking gold from the earth with every blow of the pick, each one seeming to leave a share for me. The next day when I looked for my treasure it was gone. The little box where I had put it rolled empty on the bottom of the wagon, and my coin lay hidden in the dust, miles back, up on the mountains. So we came, young, strong, healthy, hopeful, but penniless, into the new world. The nest egg was gone, but the homely bird which laid it—the power and will to work—was still there. All around us twinkled the camp fires of the new arrivals. A wilderness of canvas tents glimmered in the firelight; the men cooked and ate, played cards, drank whisky, slept rolled in their blankets, fed their teams, talked, and swore all around; and a few, less occupied than their comrades, stared at me as at a strange creature, and roused my sleeping babies, and passed them from arm to arm to have a look at such a novelty as a child.

We halted in an open space, and lighting our fire in their midst made us one with the inhabitants of Sacramento.

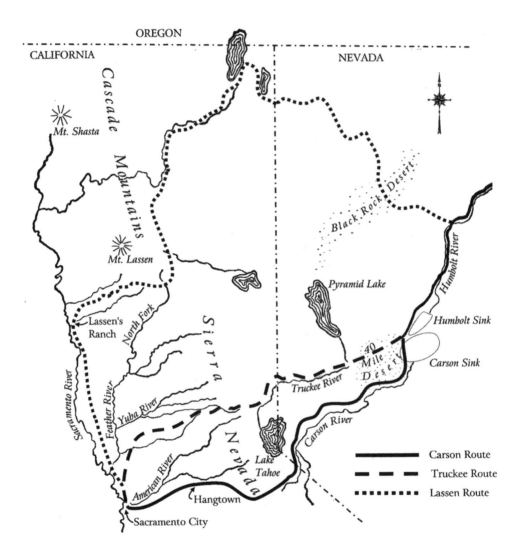

Many wagons were still on these trails in October 1849 as winter storms threatened. Travelers on the Lassen Route suffered the most because of the extra mileage and the weakened condition of both people and livestock. With the help of the government rescue parties, the last pioneers were safely off the trails by late November. Map by Bill Spurlock, drawn from George R. Stewart.

5   *At last we were near our journey's end . . .*

AFTER LONG MONTHS OF HARDSHIP, every pioneer had to face the desert which stretched out for more than forty miles beyond the Humboldt Sink in present-day western Nevada. Beyond the desert were the fearsome Sierra Nevada which posed yet another severe test for the weary forty-niners and their emaciated oxen. Most wagon trains consulted guidebooks or other travelers for strategies. There were two paths from the Humboldt Sink: the Carson Route which the Wilsons chose, and the Truckee Route a bit to the north. Either way, forty miles of desert intervened, which Luzena called "the most formidable of all the difficulties we had encountered." Few would disagree.

William Pleasants and his train debated the alternatives and decided to take the Lassen Route, which left the overland trail well before the Humboldt Sink and led northwest. Pleasants called it the Oregon Trail, but it is better known as the Lassen Route. The mountains were easier to cross via this route, but the desert was even longer—ninety miles by Pleasants' reckoning. He described the heavy toll of the ordeal:

> *The crossing of this desert occupied over fifty hours. In the passage we lost nearly half of our wagons, many of our cattle, and were compelled to abandon a large quantity of provisions. . . . Among the cattle thus lost was an old ox noted for his good sense. His owner, Sam Caldwell, had always made quite a pet of him and the two were great friends. When this faithful beast at last sank down exhausted and dying of thirst, Sam took a cup of water from his almost empty keg and attempted to revive him, at the same time calling him lovingly by name. But, too far gone to recover, the poor animal, bending his great, mournful eyes upon his master, lowed faintly in answer and expired. Sam turned sadly away, saying, 'Dear old fellow, sensible to the last.'*

The Pleasants men, father and two sons, finally reached California and halted their 162-day journey at Bidwell's Bar on the Feather River, their first home in the West.

Like the Wilsons, the Josiah and Sarah Royce family chose the Carson Route. Sarah grew up in New York State as a well-educated, deeply religious person and she kept a detailed diary of her overland trek in 1849. With husband Josiah, a farmer, and their baby Mary, Sarah traveled in the rear of the long line of immigrants that summer. They had crossed the Missouri River June 8, a full five weeks after the Wilsons.

Sarah described their desert crossing as a daunting trial. Her specific recollections are quite similar to Luzena's in most details, with one major exception: the Royces had to double back after the first fifteen miles and start over again because they made a crucial mistake as they set out onto the sand. To escape the heat of the sun they chose to travel at night, but in the darkness they failed to see the turnoff to the last spot where water and grass were available. Fifteen miles out, they realized their error. Sarah Royce recalled:

> Here we were, without water, and with only a few mouthfuls of poor feed, while our animals were already tired out, and very hungry and thirsty. No, it would be madness to go farther out into the desert under such conditions . . . Turn back! What a chill the words sent through one. . . . In all that long journey no steps ever seemed so heavy, so hard to take, as those with which I turned my back to the sun that afternoon of October 4th, 1849.[1]

They retraced their steps and found water and feed, then attempted the crossing again, this time nonstop. Like Luzena, she saw many broken-down wagons, and from one the Royces salvaged two good sides of bacon which they badly needed. When Sarah first sighted the Carson River she thought it might be a mirage, but her oxen smelled the water just as Luzena's had done and they picked up the pace to reach the riverbank.

Luzena said nothing of the arduous ascent of the Sierra after the rest at the Carson River, but George Thissell recalled in detail the difficult job of getting the wagons through:

> Here we leave the valley and climb the Sierra Nevada Mountains. No road. Not even a trail. Rocks upon rocks, steep and rough. We thought we had seen rough and rocky roads, but this was the worst we had found. . . . Where we left the canyon in the mountainside was as steep as the roof of a house. Here we put eight yoke of cattle to one wagon, though it was almost empty. . . . Our cattle, reduced to skin and bones, toiled slowly on

and up the rough ascent. Sometimes the passage between the cliffs was so narrow our wagons could scarcely pass. Often we had to lift the wagons and oxen up over the rocks that lay across the path. Many of the rocks were four and five feet high, and extended across the entire width of the canyon, consequently it was difficult to pass. We made only eight miles in one day. . . . At last we gained the summit of this outer wall, which seemed like one of nature's ramparts guarding the passage to the rich gold fields of California.

The Royces had real cause for concern as they contemplated climbing the Sierra. Winter was coming on soon and the Royces were at risk of being trapped in

Sarah Royce's diary was published after her death in 1891 by Yale University Press. Special Collections, Charles E. Young Research Library, UCLA.

Encampment at Sacramento City, November 1849. California State Library.

the snow like the Donner Party of 1846. Fortunately, they were met by a government rescue party from California October 12, which provided them with fresh mules and good advice: they must travel quickly. The Royces abandoned their wagons and packed what they could on every available animal. In one week they reached the summit and looked down upon California; scarcely two weeks later the mountain passes were completely snowed in. Had the Royces tried to travel with their wagons, they likely would have perished somewhere on the mountainside.

Luzena did not remark upon her first glimpse of California from the crest of the Sierras, but the arrival at the summit was a spiritual moment for Sarah Royce. With two-year-old Mary holding on in front of her, she rode ahead of the pack train on her borrowed white mule to see the promised land first:

California, land of sunny skies—that was my first look into your smiling face. I loved you from that moment, for you seemed to welcome me with loving look into rest and safety. However brave a face I might have put on most of the time, I knew my coward heart was yearning all the while for a home-nest and a welcome into it, and you seemed to promise me both. A short time I had on those rocks, sacred to thanksgiving and prayer; then the others came and boisterous shouts, and snatches of song made rocks and welkin [the sky] ring.

The descent into Sacramento was "tedious" for Luzena; she said they arrived in Sacramento City September 30. When Mason later applied for membership in the Society of California Pioneers, he claimed the date of his arrival in California was September 8. Both may have been right; Mason could have been citing the date they reached the summit and saw California and the downhill journey to Sacramento could have consumed three weeks. By way of comparison, Thissell said it took his group two weeks to reach Hangtown from the summit.

Before setting up camp in Sacramento City, Luzena had found her first gold by selling a batch of her biscuits to a hungry miner for a coin made of the precious metal. She quickly understood how she would find wealth in this new country. In her dreams, Luzena did not see herself digging gold out of the gravel beds. Instead, miners appeared before her, bringing gold and placing it in her hands. So it would be.

NOTES

1. Royce, *A Frontier Lady,* 45. In the 1880s, Sarah Royce's son, Josiah Jr., asked his mother to organize her diary of 1849 for his own study. He went on to become a distinguished philosopher and Harvard professor; his accomplishments were the pride of his parents and three sisters.

Luzena: SACRAMENTO CITY
1849

T HE DAYLIGHT WOKE US NEXT MORNING to the realization that if we were to accomplish anything we must be up and stirring. The world around us was all alive. Camp fires crackled, breakfast steamed, and long lines of mules and horses, packed with provisions, filed past on their way out from what was already called a city. The three or four wooden buildings and the zinc banking house, owned by Sam Brannan, looked like solid masonry beside the airy canvas structures which gleamed in the October sunshine like cloud pictures. There was no credit in '49 for men, but I was a woman with two children, and I might have bought out the town with no security other than my word. My first purchase was a quart of molasses for a dollar, and a slice of salt pork as large as my hand, for the same price. That pork, by-the-by, was an experience. When it went into the pan it was as innocent looking pork as I ever saw, but no sooner did it touch the fire than it pranced, it sizzled, frothed over the pan, sputtered, crackled, and acted as if possessed. When finally it subsided, there was left a shaving the size of a dollar, and my pork had vanished into smoke. I found afterward that many of our purchases were as deceptive, for the long trip around the "Horn" was not calculated to improve an article which was probably inferior in quality when it left New York. The flour we used was often soured and from a single sieve-full I have sifted out at one time a handful of long black worms. The butter was brown from age and had spent a year on the way out to California. I once endeavored to freshen some of this butter by washing it first in chloride of lime, and afterwards churning it with fresh milk. I improved it in a measure, for it became white, but still it retained its strength. It was, however, such a superior article to the original "Boston" butter, that my boarders ate it as a luxury. Strange to say, in a country overrun with cattle as California was in early days, fresh milk and butter were unheard of, and I sold what little milk was left from my children's meals for the enormous price of a dollar a pint. Many a sick man has come to me for a little porridge, half milk, half water, and thickened with flour, and paid me a dollar and a half a bowl full. The beans and dried fruits from Chile, and the yams and onions from the Sandwich Islands, were the best articles for table use we had for months. The New York warehouses were cleared of the provisions they had held for years, and after a twelve-months' sea voyage, they fed the hungry Californians.

Half the inhabitants kept stores; a few barrels of flour, a sack or two of yams, a keg of molasses, a barrel of salt pork, another of corned beef (like redwood in texture) some gulls' eggs from the Farallones, a sack of onions, a few picks and shovels, and a barrel of whisky, served for a stock in trade, while a board laid across the head of a barrel answered for a counter. On many counters were scales, for coin was rare, and all debts were paid in gold dust at sixteen dollars per ounce. In the absence of scales a pinch of dust was accepted as a dollar, and you may well imagine the size of the pinch very often varied from the real standard. Nothing sold for less than a dollar; it was the smallest fractional currency. A dollar each for onions, a dollar each for eggs, beef a dollar a pound, whisky a dollar a drink, flour fifty dollars a barrel. One morning an official of the town stopped at my fire, and said in his pompous way, "Madame, I want a good substantial breakfast, cooked by a woman." I asked him what he would have, and he gave his order, "Two onions, two eggs, a beef-steak and a cup of coffee." He ate it, thanked me, and gave me five dollars. The sum seems large now for such a meal, but then it was not much above cost, and if I had asked ten dollars he would have paid it.

After two or three days in Sacramento we sold our oxen, and with the proceeds, six hundred dollars, we bought an interest in the hotel kept in one of the wooden houses, a story-and-a-half building which stood on what is now know as K Street, near Sixth, close to what was then the Commercial Exchange, Board of Trade, and Chamber of Commerce, all in one "The Horse Market." The hotel we bought consisted of two rooms, the kitchen, which was my special province, and general living room, the first room I had entered in Sacramento. I thought I had already grown accustomed to the queer scenes around me, but that first glimpse into a Sacramento hotel was a picture which only loss of memory can efface. Imagine a long room, dimly lighted by dripping tallow candles stuck into whisky bottles, with bunks built from floor to ceiling on either side. A bar with rows of bottles and glasses was in one corner, and two or three miners were drinking; the barkeeper dressed in half sailor, half vaquero fashion, with a blue shirt rolled far back at the collar to display the snowy linen beneath, and his waist encircled by a flaming scarlet sash, was in commanding tones subduing their noisy demands, for the barkeeper, next to the stage-driver, was in early days the most important man in camp. In the opposite corner of the room some men were having a wordy dispute over a game of cards; a cracked fiddle was, under the manipulation of rather clumsy fingers, furnishing music for some half dozen others to dance to the tune of "Moneymusk." One young man was reading a letter by a sputtering candle, and tears rolling down his yet unbearded face told of the homesickness in his heart. Some of the men lay sick in their bunks, some lay asleep, and out from another bunk, upon this curious mingling of merriment and sadness stared the white face of a corpse. They had forgotten even to cover the still features with the edge of a blanket, and he lay there, in his rigid calmness, a silent unheeded witness to the acquired insensibility of the early settlers. What was one dead man, more or less! Nobody missed him. They would bury him tomorrow to make room for a new applicant for his bunk. The music and dancing, the card-playing, drinking, and swearing went on unchecked by the hideous presence of Death. His face grew too familiar in those days to be a terror.

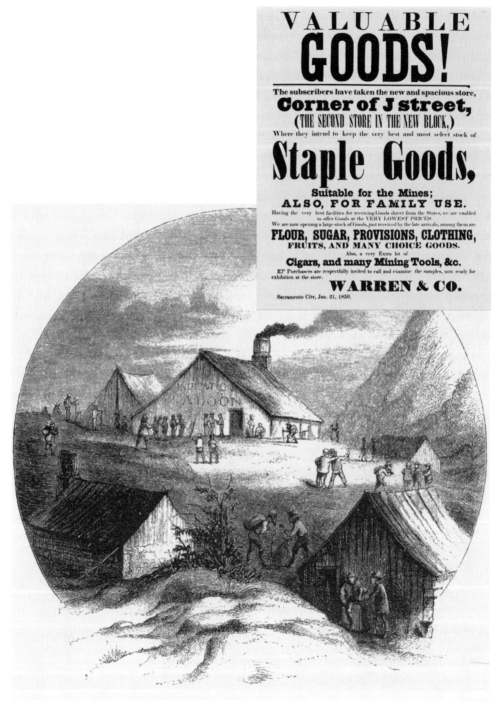

Top: *Broadside advertised the general merchandise store operated by James L. L. F. Warren and his partners in the Excelsior Tent at Mormon Bar near present day Folsom. In January 1850, they moved their business to Sacramento City. Eleanor McClatchy Collection, Sacramento Archives and Museum Collection Center.*
Bottom: *Engraving of tent settlement by J. Ross Browne for* Harper's New Monthly Magazine.

7   *The world around us was all alive . . .*

CLOSE ENCOUNTERS WITH DEATH SERVED TO FOCUS the forty-niners' thoughts on the struggle to survive. In spite of the daily stress, Luzena proved to be an astute observer. Comparisons of her recollections with other accounts not only verify her stories, but add details of life in the new California territory.

The immigrant campsites were situated mainly to the south of Sacramento City which was about a mile square. Compiling a city directory in 1850, J. Horace Culver estimated that on October 1, 1849, Luzena's first morning in town, "the population was about 2,000, wood buildings 45, cloth and tent 300, about 300 campfires, etc. in the open air and under trees."[1] Other sources put the number at 5,000, including 2,000 residents and the others transients. Still more people came as the rains of winter brought the miners down into the valley. By November 1849, Bayard Taylor, traveling reporter for the *New York Tribune,* estimated there were 10,000 people in the town. This was a phenomenal increase, considering that only 150 people lived there in April 1849. Taylor remarked, "Can the world match growth like this?"[2]

He took a stroll through the tent city, fascinated by the sights and sounds of the immigrant camp. The campsites were surrounded by brush, tree limbs, sharp ox horns, and other hazards and great care had to be taken to avoid injury. He thought he had never seen "such worn, weather-beaten individuals" as the newly-arrived pioneers. In the early evenings they would gather around campfires to share stories of the overland journey, play card games, or drink together:

> *The conversation, however, was sure to wind up with a talk about home—a lamentation for its missed comforts and frequently a regret at having forsaken them. The subject was inexhaustible.*

Listening to this talk made even the optimistic Mr. Taylor feel homesick. Others were disgusted by Sacramento. Jonas Winchester was one of many miners who took shelter there for the winter of 1849–1850. He wrote to his beloved Susan:

> *Most of the stores and houses are without floors, with canvas roofs and walls. No building is enclosed by a fence; but all are, as it were, in one immense open lot, one great cesspool of mud, offal, garbage, dead animals, and that worst of nuisances consequent upon the entire absence of outhouses. I cannot describe it as it is, but it is desolate beyond description.*[3]

To house the burgeoning population and provide the necessities, buildings sprouted in profusion and confusion. During the fall of 1849, two zinc-covered buildings appeared; a warehouse slightly north of the town and a house on J Street. One of these was probably the zinc building Luzena remembered as a bank owned by Sam Brannan. There were also a few brick structures, but wood was the most common material for the upscale builder. Carpenters earned $16 per day, and ordinary laborers were paid $1.00 or $1.50 per hour and they were incessantly busy. At Christmas, Dr. Israel Lord, a homeopathic physician from Aurora, Illinois, wrote in his diary that in the one week he had been in the city, "fifty buildings of considerable dimensions have been reared," and the town had "an active business appearance."[4] Bayard Taylor thought the business prospects were excellent.

The Wilsons moved quickly to launch their first venture, a hotel at Sixth and K Streets that competed with other boarding houses built that year. Their hotel, called the Trumbow House, was situated at present-day 502 K Street. It was a rough and tumble establishment according to Luzena's description. Sam Brannan's City Hotel, Sacramento's first, had been completed that summer, but accommodations for travelers who could afford to pay were far from lavish. Musician and actor Stephen Massett was an early guest, and he described his room:

> *The heat was insufferable, mosquitoes were buzzing about, and with their slow though sure attendants, fleas, and bedbugs came in myriads to greet and congratulate me upon my arrival. Scratching and itching, itching and scratching, kept me pretty well awake all night; and then the stifled smell—the noise inside and out—the swearing and snoring of the occupants, the barking of dogs, the leaving of numberless trains of mules and donkeys outside, the cries of children, rendered the scene a perfect pandemonium—and to crown the whole, just as I had managed from sheer exhaustion to 'drop off into a doze,'*

William G. Johnston's overland company was, he claimed, the first to arrive in Sacramento in 1849. This illustration of the rough hotel accommodations appeared in his book, Overland to California, *published in 1892. California State Library.*

I felt a heavy bump come up against the slender board that screened me from the street—when to my astonishment the head of a big ox presented itself, and with its cold and moist snout commenced rubbing against my knee![6]

To purchase a stake in the hotel business, Mason and Luzena sold their oxen. The usual venue for such transactions was the Horse Market that Luzena mentioned which was nearby on K Street. The market was structured quite simply: no rules, no formal hours and no guarantees. Many men sold their own livestock, preferring not to pay a percentage of the sale to a hired auctioneer. A seller would tether his oxen in the sales area under a huge oak where he could take bids, working hard to ensure he was heard over the voices of other auctioneers who were working the crowd simultaneously. As always, the buyer had to beware. Potential purchasers often looked long and hard at the animals on sale, sometimes pausing for thirty minutes between successive bids. Mason got $600 for his oxen, and most likely the new owners put the animals to work again immediately, hauling freight.

Much has been written of the high cost of living in early California, and Luzena's recall of her purchases is typical. She was living on a strict budget and bought few luxuries. As a working mother, she had little time to tour the town and partake of all that was offered. But Bayard Taylor, a single man on an expense account, dined well and even gained weight on meals of salmon, trout, elk and venison. Fresh produce was a rarity, so a man like John Schwartz could make $25,000 in just one summer by selling vegetables from his farm located across the river from Sacramento. Luzena said that "half the inhabitants kept

George V. Cooper's lithograph gives a detailed view of the booming young city in December 1849. Sutter's Fort is located in the distance, about 2.5 miles to the east, at present-day 26th and K Streets. California State Library.

stores," and presumably the other half were buying; thus, a great deal of money was always changing hands. Much of the gold that came out of the mines was consumed by the local economy as the miners soon discovered. Luzena remembered that everything cost at least a dollar but she may not have been entirely correct. According to Sacramento's first historian, typical 1849 prices were as follows: beef, 15 cents per pound; bread, 50 cents per loaf; butter, $2.50 to $3.00 per pound; cheese, $1.50 per pound; milk, $1.00 per quart; dried apples, $1.00 to $2.00 per pound; saleratus [baking soda], $6.00 per pound.[6]

Luzena's homemaking skills were in demand in the West, and she could command a good price for her labor. In 1849, most of the men were recently separated from their families and were homesick. Doing business with a woman and savoring her meals was a pleasure to them. Thus, managing a hotel or boarding house was a common occupation for a respectable Western woman in those days. Luzena, like many of her gender, was quick to realize the business advantages of being female, such as the availability of credit. A woman could get paid for cooking, cleaning, sewing and doing laundry; this was a new economic reality! Luzena was able to make money just as easily as Mason could, and she began to see herself as a businesswoman in her own right. So with eyes wide open to the harsh realities glimpsed in that memorable room on K Street, Luzena began managing her first California hotel. She would remain in the hotel business for the next twenty-five years.

NOTES

1. Mead J. Kibbey, *Horace Culver's Sacramento City Directory for the year 1851,* 268.
2. Bayard Taylor, *Eldorado: Adventures in the Path of Empire,* 176.
3. Jonas Winchester Letters 1849–1853, *Golden Notes,* 6.
4. Israel Shipman Pelton Lord, *At the Extremity of Civilization,* 197, 281.
5. Stephen C. Massett, *Drifting About: or What Jeems Pipes of Pipesville Saw—and Did,* 125.
6. John F. Morse, *History of Sacramento,* 38.

Luzena: SACRAMENTO CITY
Late 1849

I T WAS A MOTLEY CROWD THAT GATHERED EVERY DAY at my table but always at my coming the loud voices were hushed, the swearing ceased, the quarrels stopped, and deference and respect were as readily and as heartily tendered me as if I had been a queen. I was a queen. Any woman who had a womanly heart, who spoke a kindly, sympathetic word to the lonely, homesick men, was a queen, and lacked no honor which a subject could bestow. Women were scarce in those days. I lived six months in Sacramento and saw only two. There may have been others, but I never saw them. There was no time for visiting or gossiping; it was hard work from daylight till dark, and sometimes long after, and I nodded to my neighbor and called out "Good morning" as each of us hung the clothes out to dry on the lines. Yes, we worked; we did things that our high-toned servants would now look at aghast, and say it was impossible for a woman to do. But the one who did not work in '49 went to the wall. It was a hand to hand fight with starvation at the first; later the "flush" times came, when the mines had given out their golden store, and every one had money.

Many a miserable unfortunate, stricken down by the horrors of scurvy or Panama fever, died in his lonely, deserted tent, and waited days for the hurrying crowd to bestow the rites of burial. It has been a life-long source of regret to me that I grew hard-hearted like the rest. I was hard-worked, hurried all day, and tired out, but I might have stopped sometimes for a minute to heed the moans which caught my ears from the canvas house next to me. I knew a young man lived there, for he had often stopped to say "Good morning," but I thought he had friends in the town; and when I heard his weak calls for water I never thought but some one gave it. One day the moans ceased, and, on looking in, I found him lying dead with not even a friendly hand to close his eyes. Many a time since, when my own boys have been wandering in new countries have I wept for the sore heart of that poor boy's mother, and I have prayed that if ever want and sickness came to mine, some other woman would be more tender than I had been, and give them at least a glass of cold water.

We lived two months in the "Trumbow House," then sold our interest in it for a thousand dollars in dust, and left it, moving a few doors below on K Street. The street was always full of wagons and pack-mules; five hundred would often pass in a day packed heavily with picks, shovels, camp-kettles, gum-boots, and provisions for the miners. A fleet of schooners and sloops anchored at the river bank was always unloading the freight from San Francisco. Steam-vessels had not yet plowed the muddy waters of the Sacramento. When one of these slow-moving schooners brought the Eastern mails there was excitement in the town. For the hour all work was suspended, and every man dropped into line to ask in turn for letters from home. Sometimes the letters came; more often the poor fellows turned away with pale faces and sick disappointment in their hearts. Even the fortunate recipients of the precious sheets seemed often not less sad, for the closely written lines brought with their loving words a host of tender memories, and many a man whose daily life was one long battle faced with fortitude and courage, succumbed at the gentle touch of the home letters and wept like a woman. There was never a jeer at these sacred tears, for each man respected, nay, honored the feelings of his neighbor. Brave, honest, noble men! The world will never see the like again of those "pioneers of '49." They were, as a rule, upright, energetic, and hard-working, many of them men of education and culture whom the misfortune of poverty had forced into the ranks of labor in this strange country. The rough days which earned for California its name for recklessness had not begun. There was no shooting, little gambling, and less theft in those first months. The necessities of hard work left no leisure for the indulgence even of one's temper, and the "rough" element which comes to every mining country with the first flush times had not yet begun to crowd the West.

One of the institutions of '49, which more than filled the place of our present local telegraphic and telephonic systems, was the "Town Crier." Every pioneer must remember his gaunt form, unshaven face, and long, unkempt hair, and his thin bob-tailed, sorrel Mexican pony, and the clang of his bell as he rode through the streets and cried his news. Sometimes he announced a "preaching," or a "show," "mail in," an "auction," or a "stray." Another of the features of the city was the horse market to which I have already alluded. A platform was built facing what was only by courtesy called the street, and from his elevation every day rang out the voice of the auctioneer and around it gathered the men who came to buy or sell. The largest trade of the day was in live stock. The miners who came down with dust exchanged it here for horses and mules to carry back their supplies, and vaqueros brought in their cattle to sell to the city butchers. Here, too, were sold the hay and grain, which almost brought their weight in gold.

The population of Sacramento was largely a floating one. Today there might be ten thousand people in the town, and tomorrow four thousand of them might be on their way to the gold fields. The immigrants came pouring in every day from the plains, and schooners from San Francisco brought a living freight, eager to be away to the mountains.

Gambling houses lured a diverse clientele, as shown in this sketch of the El Dorado Saloon in Sacramento, published by the Illustrated London News *in June 1852. Then, as now, elaborate decor, music, and drink helped entertain patrons as they parted with their gold. California State Library.*

9 A hand to hand fight with starvation . . .

I N THIS "FLOATING" POPULATION, LUZENA RECALLED SEEING only two women; of course, there were more than that around. One man wrote home that "it is quite a novel sight to see a lady on the street."[1] Nonetheless, the *Placer Times* of Sacramento recorded details of the White–Kewen wedding December 15, 1849, noting that twenty women attended. Earlier in the year, eighteen women had attended an Independence Day gala. But the immigrant women in the town and tent camps, like Luzena, probably had little time to attend such celebrations. Bayard Taylor openly admired the stoic strength of the female pioneers: "The women who had come by the overland route appeared to have stood the hardships of the journey remarkably well, and were not half so loud as the men in their complaints."

Some of the women in town were pursuing other lines of work. The Eagle Theater featured the "celebrated actress Mrs. Ray" who earned the handsome sum of $200 a week, although her acting skills were meager, according to Taylor, an acid-tongued drama critic:

> *Several acts are filled with the usual amount of fighting and terrible speeches. . . . Mrs. Ray rushes in and throws herself into an attitude in the middle of the stage: why she does it, no one can tell. This movement, which she repeats several times . . . has no connection with the tragedy; it is evidently introduced for the purpose of showing the audience that there is, actually, a female performer. The miners, to whom the sight of a woman is not a frequent occurrence, are delighted with these passages and applaud vehemently.*

Women could also be found working in the many gambling houses and brothels, but wages for these sporting women and prostitutes are hard to determine. Female musicians, however, sometimes entertained in these establishments, and Taylor said one "Swiss-organ girl" made $4,000 in about six months as a saloon musician.

As Luzena said, every man and woman had to work to survive in early California. But even diligent labor could not guard against all risks. Doctors reported that diarrhea, fevers, typhus and dysentery were common in the city. The pioneers also brought with them the dreaded cholera which had claimed many lives on both the overland and the sea routes. The low standard of sanitation intensified the spread of contagious diseases. One early historian noted, "The mortality in the city was very great during November 1849, reaching some days to the number of 20."[2] Flies, mosquitoes and fleas were present in great numbers. Drinking water was drawn from the river and distributed throughout the city by wagon, and bathing was uncommon. A quick swim in the river usually was deemed sufficient.

There was widespread tragedy, especially among immigrants whose health and personal resources were exhausted by the journey west. Luzena mourned the lonely death of the young man in the next tent and regretted her hardheartedness in ignoring his cries. Such self-centered behavior was seen often. A son might abandon his father, or a brother leave his brother in the mad rush. People grew accustomed to death during their travels to the new world and were undeterred by it once they arrived. Nonetheless, most survived the arduous conditions.

The Odd Fellows and the Masonic Lodges of Sacramento did charitable work and attempted to relieve the sufferings of their fellow man by providing funds to bury the dead as well as meeting urgent requests for food and lodging. Although their volunteer efforts fell far short of the need, they demonstrated that not everyone was unfeeling and uninvolved.

Luzena openly praised the men she met on the trail and in Sacramento. Their courtesy and consideration warmed her heart and their work ethic gained her respect. She was not blind to their "acquired insensibility" toward their fellow man, but she forgave their shortcomings, seeing the same flaw develop in herself. But not everyone admired the character of the new Californians. Dr. Israel Lord, a fellow immigrant, was a pious Baptist who found both the town and its inhabitants disorderly. He was appalled that so few attended Bible study and, as an ardent advocate of temperance, strongly disapproved of all the drinking and swearing around him:

> *Gambling seems to be the business, not the pleasure of this place. . . . Occasionally*
> *you will find a man of mind, a moral and intellectual man; but they, few or many, are*

hidden, overwhelmed by the putrid tide whose impurity would . . . push the reeking impieties of Sodom a backward step from Hell.

In contrast, Luzena thought there was "little gambling" and saw the men as stalwarts confronting a great challenge. Dr. Lord seemed predisposed to judge harshly, while Luzena wanted to see the good in her fellow man; their perspectives were as different as their characters. Not surprisingly, Dr. Lord left California to return home; Luzena stayed.

Even while blasting away at the forty-niners, Dr. Lord admitted that he had never lived any place where thievery was so rare, a fact Luzena also noted. This happy state of affairs would not last, and in years to come the miners would wax nostalgic about the early code of honor which was their form of self-government. By 1852 many miners felt too much civilization had already destroyed their idyllic frontier life.

Indeed, the trappings of society arrived quickly at Sacramento. A post office was in place by July 1849 and mail was eagerly awaited. If they missed hearing the mail call from the town crier, immigrants could check the weekly newspaper, the *Placer Times,* for a list of people for whom letters were waiting. Messages were sent to anxious families back home, some of them relaying sad news of loved

Sacramento viewed from the river in 1849. Private collection.

This lettersheet, used by the miners as stationery, depicts the difficulties of travel during the winter months. The flow of goods to the mines slowed considerably since supply wagon trains could not get through. The resultant shortages and higher prices forced many miners down into the valley for the duration. California State Library.

ones who had died on the way. For entertainment there was always a gambling house or the Eagle Theater down on the wharf.

Luzena recalled only sailing ships anchored along the river; but, in reality, steamships arrived in Sacramento before she did. Although the first steamer docked there in August 1849, regular steamer service didn't start until October. The steamers were faster and soon took over the river routes. Depending on the wind, a sailing ship might take three to ten days to make the San Francisco–Sacramento run; a steamer could make it in ten to twelve hours. Business was booming; people stood in line to pay $30 for the trip with no meals included.[3] In addition to human cargo, ships brought in all manner of goods for sale in the city and the mining regions. Dr. Lord provided a vivid description of the Sacramento Wharf:

> *A tangled mess of Mexicans, Chinese, Chileans, and Kanakas [Hawaiians]; also horses, mules, asses, oxen, drays and lumber, flour, potatoes, molasses, brandy, pickles, oysters, jam, cabbages, books, furniture and almost everything that one can think of.*

From the wharf the freight was transported overland by oxen-drawn wagons or pack mules. Teamsters made good money. In December 1849, a wagon owner could charge $50 to haul one hundred pounds of freight from Sacramento to Mormon Island near present-day Folsom. Luzena said the "streets were always full" of this traffic. Thus, the busy thoroughfares were extremely dusty in summer and in the rainy season became a perfect quagmire.

Commerce grew throughout the city. Musician–entertainer Stephen Massett was first lured to Sacramento by Sam Brannan's offer of a job as an auctioneer. Massett presided at numerous sales in the town and at Sutter's Fort, always entertaining the crowd as he sold the merchandise. Summing up the life of a young California entrepreneur, he wrote: "In those days everyone was crazy—money came and went—went and came—you knew not how and cared not where—from morning till night it was one scene of excitement and frenzy!"

NOTES

1. Edwin G. Hall letter, October 26, 1849, California State Library.
2. Mead J. Kibbey, *Horace Culver's Sacramento City Directory for the year 1851,* 268.
3. Alexander J. Dickie, "Early San Francisco Shipping," *Pacific Marine Review,* 96.

Luzena: SACRAMENTO CITY
Winter 1849–1850

There was not much lumber in Sacramento, and what little there was, and the few wooden houses, came in ships around the Horn from Boston. The great majority of the people lived like ourselves in houses made of canvas, and with natural dirt floors. The furniture was primitive: a stove (of which there always seemed plenty), a few cooking vessels, a table made of unplaned boards, two or three boxes which answered for chairs, and a bunk built in the corner to hold our mattresses and blankets. One of the articles on which great profit was made was barley, and my husband had invested our little fortune of a thousand dollars in that commodity at fifteen cents a pound, and this lay piled at the wind side of the house as a additional protection. The first night we spent in our new home it rained and we slept with a cotton umbrella, a veritable pioneer, spread over our heads to keep off the water. For days it rained incessantly; the streets ran full of water. Men and animals struggled through a sea of mud. We wrung out our blankets every morning, and warmed them by the fire—they never had time to dry. The canvas roof seemed like a sieve, and water dropped on us through every crevice.

At last the clouds broke, the sun shone out, the rain ceased, and the water began to sink away and give us a glimpse of mother earth, and everybody broke out into smiles and congratulations over the change. One afternoon late, about Christmas—I do not remember the exact day—as I was cooking supper and the men were coming in from work, the familiar clang of the Crier's bell was heard down the street, and as he galloped past, the cry, "The levee's broke" fell on our ears. We did not realize what that cry foretold, but knew that it was misfortune that was mutual, and one that every man must fight; so my husband ran like the rest to the Point, a mile or more away up the American River, where the temporary sand-bag barrier had given way. Every man worked with beating heart and hurrying breath to save the town, but it was useless; their puny strength could do nothing against such a flood of waters. At every moment the breech grew wider, and the current stronger, and they hastened back to rescue the threatened property. In the meantime I went on cooking supper, the children played about on the floor, and I stepped every minute to the door and looked up the street for some one to come back to tell me of the break.

While I stood watching, I saw tiny rivulets trickling over the ground, and behind them came the flood of waters in such a volume that it had not time to spread, but seemed like a little wall three or four inches high. Almost before I thought what it was, the water rushed against the door-sill at my feet and five minutes more it rose over this small obstacle and poured on the floor. I snatched up the children, and put them on the bed, and hastily gathered up the articles which I feared the water might reach. The water kept rising, and I concluded to carry my children into the hotel, which we had lately sold, and which stood some three or four feet above the ground. I put them inside the door, and ran back, meeting my husband just come from the levee. He said, "We must sleep in there tonight" and, knowing the scanty hotel accommodations, I gathered up our beds and blankets and carried them in, and put in a basket the supper I had just cooked. By this time the water was six inches high in our house, and I knew we could not come back for some days, so I gathered up what I could of our clothing, and hurried again to the hotel through water which now reached nearly to my knees and ran with a force which almost carried me off my feet. In an hour more the whole town was afloat, and the little boats were rowed here and there picking up the people and rescuing what could be saved of the property. It was not until later in the night that we began to feel real alarm, for we expected every hour to see the water subside, but it steadily rose, and at midnight we moved to the upper floor. All through the night came the calls for "Help! help!" from every quarter, and the men listened a moment and then rowed in the direction of the call sometimes too late to save. The cruel clouds clung like a cloak over the moon, and refused to break and give them light to aid them in their search. Sometimes for a moment the light shone through, but only long enough to make the darkness blacker. And the waters rushed and roared, and pale, set faces peered into the darkness, upon the hurrying monster which swallowed up in its raging fury the results of their hard labors and their perseverance.

The place where we had taken refuge was one long room, a half story with a window at each end; and here for several days lived forty people. There was one other woman besides myself and my two children; all the rest were men. For provisions, we caught the sacks of onions or boxes of anything which went floating by, or fished up with boat-hooks whatever we could. The fire by which we cooked was built of driftwood. Those were days of terror and fear, for at every minute we expected to follow the zinc house we saw float away on the flood. The water splashed upon the ceiling below, and the rain and the wind made the waves run high on this inland sea. The crazy structure shook and trembled at every blast of wind or rush of water, but the swiftest current turned away and left us standing. They hung a blanket across one corner of the room, and that little territory, about six feet by four, was mine exclusively during our stay. The rest of the space was common property, where we cooked and ate during the day, and at night the men slept on the floor, rolled in their blankets. Two or three boats were tied always at the windows, and the men rowed out to the river and back again, bringing provisions from the store hulks, and news from the people who had taken refuge on the vessels lying there. It came to be a horrible suspense, waiting either for the expected destruction or watching for the first abating of the waters. Even now, more than thirty years after, I can not hear the sound of continuous rain without, in a measure, living over again the terrors of those monotonous days, and feel creeping over me the dread of the rising waters.

Many an occurrence of those terrible days would have been funny, had we not been so filled with fear, and had not tragedy trodden so closely on the heels of comedy. Heroic actions went unnoticed and uncounted. Every man was willing, and many times did risk his life to aid his neighbor. Many a poor fellow doubtless found his death in the waters, and his grave far out at sea, perhaps in the lonely marshes which lined the river banks. There were few close ties and few friendships; and when a familiar face dropped out no one knew whether the man was dead or gone away; nobody inquired, nobody cared. The character of the pioneers was a paradox. They were generous to a degree which we can scarcely realize, yet selfish beyond parallel.

One of the numerous queer accessories of our flood-surrounded household was the gentlemen's dressing-room. If there had been any one there to see, it must have been a very remarkable performance. Each man took his bundle of clothing, brought from the schooners, and rowing to the corner of the house, climbed up to the peak of the roof, where, at his leisure, and in a dexterously acrobatic way, he re-arranged his toilet and cast his insect-infested clothing into the flood. Inside the house the scenes were quite as remarkable. We had all professions among our number: lawyers, physicians, miners, mechanics, merchants. Some had been senators, some gamblers; some had been owners of great plantations in the South; some had shipped before the mast. And they talked in groups about the fire, told stories, sang—rarely some one played melancholy tunes on a sad violin—played cards, gathered drift-wood, and sawed and split it up, dried their wet garments by the fire, and watched for the turning of the flood. At the end of ten days the change came; and at the end of the seventeenth day the water had run down to wading depth and we left the hotel.

The fastenings of the canvas of our house had broken away, but by some good fortune it still clung to the slender scantlings, so we had the beginnings of a house. Between the supports had gathered great piles of drift-wood and the carcasses of several animals; in one corner lay our rusty stove, the whole covered with slime and sediment. My husband cleared out the small enclosure, fastened down the canvas walls, and built a floating floor, which rose and sank with the tide, and at every footstep the water splashed up through the open cracks. We walked on a plank from the floor to the beds, under which hung great sheets of mould. At night, when I awoke, I reached down the bed-post till my hand touched the water, and if it had risen above a certain notch, we got up and packed our movables, in preparation for a new misfortune; if it was still below the notch, we went to sleep again. A boat was tied always at the door, ready to carry us away, and we lived in this way for six weeks in constant anticipation of another overflow. The canvas city was laid low; the wooden houses stood like grim sentinels in the waste, and slime and drift-wood covered the whole town. The flood of '49, I have been told, was not nearly so high as that of '52, and probably wrecked a far smaller quantity of property, but it was an unexpected blow to the '49ers, and therefore carried with it everything they had. There was not protection of any kind for property. The canvas which covered their scanty stores of goods was no barrier agains the inroads of that ocean.

No attempt had been made to ward off the effects of so fearful and powerful an enemy, and the survivors were left, as we were, adrift without a dollar. When the mule trains began to move again, the poor beasts would flounder out of one hole into another, miring sometimes half up to their sides, and would be packed and unpacked half a dozen times in the length of as many blocks. Our little fortune of barley was gone—the sacks had burst and grain had sprouted—and ruin stared us again in the face. We were terrified at the awful termination of the winter, and I felt that I should never again be safe unless high in the Sierra. A new excitement came whispered down from the mountains, that they had "struck it rich" at Nevada City—for every group of three or four tents was called a city— so we made up our minds that we would try the luck of the new mining camp. But how to get there? That was the question. We had neither money nor wagons, and apparently no way to get them. Finally we found a man with an idle team, who said he would take us, that is myself and the two children, and a stove and two sacks of flour, to Nevada City for seven hundred dollars. This looked hopeless, and I told him I guessed we wouldn't go as we had no money. I must have carried my honesty in my face, for he looked at me a minute and said, "I'll take you, Ma'am, if you will go security for the money." I promised him it should be paid, "if I lived, and we made the money." So, pledged to a new master, Debt, we pressed forward on the road. It took us twelve long days and nights to traverse the distance of sixty miles, from Sacramento to Nevada City. There were no roads and the track, well nigh effaced by the winter storms, led up and down steep mountains, across deep ravines, through marshy holes, and over mountain streams. We were away from any shelter, for the way was as desolate as if the foot of man had never trod the soil. Scarce a sound broke the stillness of the nights except the sighing of the pines, the crash of a falling tree, or the howling of a panther. Sometimes we were overtaken by mule trains which passed us and vanished into the woods like phantoms. Occasionally we came across a lonely prospector, bending over his rocker, watching with eager eyes for the precious dust; but like a spirit, he presently dropped out of sight, and we were again alone.

The winter rains and melting snows had saturated the earth like a sponge, and the wagon and oxen sunk like lead in the sticky mud. Sometimes a whole day was consumed in going two or three miles, and one day we made camp but a quarter of a mile distant from the last. The days were spent in digging out both animals and wagon, and the light of the camp fire was utilized to mend the broken bolts and braces. We built the fire at night close by the wagon, under which we slept, for it had no cover. To add to the miseries of the trip it rained, and one night when the wagon was mired, and we could not shelter under it, we slept with our feet pushed under it and the old cotton umbrella spread over our faces. Sometimes, as we went down the mountains, they were so steep we tied great trees behind to keep the wagon from falling over the oxen; and once when the whole surface of the mountain side was a smooth, slippery rock, the oxen stiffened out their legs, and wagon and all literally slid down a quarter of a mile. But the longest way has an end. At last we caught the glimmer of the miners' huts far down in the gulch and reached the end of our journey.

Detail of the Casilear and Bainbridge lithograph of the January 1850 flood in Sacramento shows submerged businesses along Front Street in the foreground. K Street runs diagonally from lower right to upper left. Flood waters appear fairly shallow in this part of town, but depths of ten to twenty feet were reported in low lying areas. California Historical Society.

11   *The dread of the rising waters . . .*

T HERE IS NO DOUBT THAT THE WINTER OF 1849–1850 was unusually wet. Dr. Thomas Logan dutifully recorded a total rainfall of thirty-six inches, more than double the usual seventeen inches. The rains began in October and fell steadily until about Christmas time. Many miners descended from the Sierras to spend the winter in Sacramento City. Jonas Winchester slogged to town through the mud and rain and wrote to his wife Susan:

> *It was the hardest time I ever had in my life. My feet soaking wet from daylight till dark and pantaloons ditto to my thighs. I have seen something of California life in four short months, but this rainy season caps all for discomfort and desolation.*

That grim day, November 19, 1849, was both his thirty-ninth birthday and his fourteenth wedding anniversary.

According to Luzena, the Wilson family spent October and November in the Trumbow House, which is spelled Trumbo in the 1851 city directory. They moved into their tent dwelling in December, a month of steady rain. With the proceeds from the sale of the hotel, they bought barley, more than 6,000 pounds of it by her calculations; barley was a popular feed for mules and therefore quite saleable.

In late December, the rains finally eased and a spell of balmy weather delighted the pioneers. However, the warmer temperatures began to melt the snowpack and the rivers, already full, overflowed their banks. On January 9, 1850, the flood that Luzena so vividly described engulfed the town. While she ran to take her two boys to shelter in the Trumbow House, everyone else in town was scrambling to find safety as well.

Sarah Royce, whose family had walked the same overland trail as Luzena's, found herself in the same flood waters. The Royces had arrived in Sacramento on New Year's Day, coming down from the mining camp at Weaver Creek near Hangtown, which had been their home for two months. They planned to open a general store in the city. Once again, Sarah's story verified Luzena's. The Royces first took shelter in the second story of a nearby house where she and her daughter were given a partitioned corner as their own bedroom. Soon more than fifty men crowded in as the water rose. The winds and waves terrified them all, but their structure, like the Trumbow House, also stood. Rowboats passed by regularly, providing news and supplies. After six days, though, the Royces decided to abandon Sacramento entirely, took a rowboat to the wharf, and boarded a steamer for San Francisco. Their residency in Sacramento lasted only fifteen days.

Many women in Sacramento took boat passage to the Bay to escape the flood. Stephen Massett, ever cheerful, rowed to the home of friends, planning to rescue the ladies there. His boat passed through the open doors of the house and came alongside the piano, which was submerged up to the keys. Reveling in his latest adventure, Massett was delighted to find a copy of his own musical composition, *When the Moon on the Lake is Beaming*, floating atop the water! He thought that "everybody seemed jolly" as they drifted about in the clear moonlight, salvaging whatever was carried by on the current. He corroborated Luzena's recollections about life on the rooftops:

> *Those persons who were lucky enough to own a house lived and slept on the roof— cooked on the roof—made calls on the roof—drank on the roof—prayed on the roof— laughed and joked on the roof—sang on the roof—took a bath on the roof—cursed the gold fields on the roof—wished they were back in New York on the roof—got married on the roof— wrote letters on the roof—and thought they'd never get off the roof!*

The Wilson's prized "mulley" cow survived the flood, although Luzena did not say how. Many cows, horses, mules and oxen drowned, but some made it to the river banks where they stood in the water for days. A few men began to rescue them in boats and ferry the poor beasts to higher ground at the city cemetery near present-day Tenth and Broadway. James Eaton participated in the livestock rescue aboard a boat that could hold a dozen animals at a time. He wrote, "It seemed as if the stock understood that we were trying to help them and they offered no resistance whatsoever . . . they would stand perfectly still on the boat."[1] Eventually all these surviving animals were driven from the cemetery to Sutter's Fort where some pasture was available for them. How the beasts were reunited with their owners remains a mystery. Many property owners had to pay salvage for the return of their goods and merchandise; fifty percent of the value was a common charge. Perhaps the livestock rescuers charged a fee for their services, too. In any case, Luzena's cow was an experienced swimmer after crossing many rivers in the overland trek; her survival skills were likewise well-honed.

Although surprisingly few people drowned, many lost all their possessions; and an enormous amount of merchandise was ruined. The survivors suffered

The multi-talented Stephen Massett included witty sketches like this in his 1863 book, Drifting About. Fairfield Public Library.

physically and financially. Overworked doctors struggled to minister to the sick who were already under care, and more illness resulted from exposure to the elements. The cost of living rose sharply in the days after the flood, which made life even more difficult for those in precarious circumstances.

The Wilsons lost their barley investment and had to begin again. Luzena reckoned that they sheltered in the hotel for seventeen days, which puts their return to the tent on January 26. They lived with the mold, slime and smell of the city for another six weeks before setting their sights on the goldfields of the Sierra. They were attracted to a settlement soon to be named Nevada City, where miners had begun prospecting around September 1849. Much of the activity was centered on two ravines called Gold Run and Deer Creek. On the hills above these ravines more gold was being taken from the Coyote Diggings. Mason and Luzena weren't the only ones to respond to news of the find; by the time they got to the camp, hundreds of men were pouring in to claim a share of the wealth. So, muddy, hopeful and in debt, the Wilsons arrived at their new home in early March 1850.

NOTES

1.   James Eaton, "From the memoirs of James Eaton," *Golden Notes,* Summer, 6.

Luzena: NEVADA CITY
1850

FROM THE BROW OF A STEEP MOUNTAIN we caught the first glimpse of a mining camp. Nevada City, a row of canvas tents lining each of the two ravines, which, joining, emptied into Deer Creek, lay at our feet, flooded with the glory of the spring sunshine. The gulches seemed alive with moving men. Great, brawny miners wielded the pick and shovel, while others stood knee deep in the icy water, and washed the soil from the gold. Every one seemed impelled by the frenzy of fever as men hurried here and there, so intent upon their work they had scarcely time to breathe. Our entrance into the busy camp could not be called a triumphal one, and had there been a "back way" we should certainly have selected it. Our wagon wheels looked like solid blocks; the color of the oxen was indistinguishable, and we were mud from head to foot. I remember filling my wash-basin three times with fresh water before I had made the slightest change apparent in the color of my face; and I am sure I scrubbed till my arms ached, before I got the children back to their natural hue. We were not rich enough to indulge in the luxury of a canvas home; so a few pine boughs and branches of the undergrowth were cut and thrown into a rude shelter for the present, and my husband hurried away up the mountain to begin to split out "shakes" for a house. Since our experience of rain in Sacramento, we were inclined to think that rain was one of the daily or at least weekly occurrences of a California spring, and the first precaution was to secure a water-tight shelter. Our bedding was placed inside the little brush house, my cook stove set up near it under the shade of a great pine tree, and I was established, without further preparation, in my new home. When I was left alone in the afternoon—it was noon when we arrived—I cast my thoughts about me for some plan to assist in the recuperation of the family finances. As always occurs to the mind of a woman, I thought of taking boarders. There was already a thriving establishment of the kind just down the road, under the shelter of a canvas roof, as was set forth by its sign in lamp-black on a piece of cloth: "Wamac's Hotel. Meals $1.00."

I determined to set up a rival hotel. So I bought two boards from a precious pile belonging to a man who was building the second wooden house in town. With my own hands I chopped stakes, drove them into the ground, and set up my table. I bought provisions at a neighboring store, and when my husband came back at night he found, mid the weird light of the pine torches, twenty miners eating at my table. Each man as he rose put a dollar in my hand and said I might count him as a permanent customer. I called my hotel "El Dorado."

From the first day it was well patronized, and I shortly after took my husband into partnership. The miners were glad to get something to eat, and were always willing to pay for it. As in Sacramento, goods of all kinds sold at enormous figures, but, as no one ever hesitated to buy on that account, dealers made huge profits. The most rare and costly articles of luxury were fruits and vegetables. One day that summer an enterprising pioneer of agricultural tastes brought in a wagon load of watermelons and sold them all for an ounce (sixteen dollars) each. I bought one for the children and thought no more of the price than one does now of buying a dish of ice-cream. Peaches sold at from one to two dollars each and were miserable apologies for fruit at that. Potatoes were a dollar a pound and for a time even higher. As the days progressed we prospered. In six weeks we had saved money enough to pay the man who brought us up from Sacramento the seven hundred dollars we owed him. In a little time, the frame of a house grew up around me, and presently my cook stove and brush house were enclosed under a roof. This house was gradually enlarged room by room, to afford accommodation for our increasing business. One Sunday afternoon as a great recreation, I took a walk along the mountainside above the town, now grown to be of some size. Looking down I found it necessary to ask which was my own house, for I had never before seen the outside of it at any considerable distance. We had then from seventy-five to two hundred boarders at twenty-five dollars a week. I became luxurious and hired a cook and waiters. Maintaining only my position as managing housekeeper, I retired from active business in the kitchen.

The "Coyote Diggings," for that was the early name of the Nevada City placer mines, were very rich in coarse gold, and money came pouring into the town. Everybody had money, and everybody spent it. Money ran through one's fingers like water through a sieve. The most profitable employment of the time was gambling, and fifty or sixty of the men who pursued the profession were guests at my table. Many of them made fortunes and retired into a quieter and less notorious life. Of them all I can now remember only one—Billy Briggs, who has grown to prominence in San Francisco. I see him now, portly, swarthy, and complacent, and wonder what has become of the slender, fair-complexioned, smooth-faced, gentlemanly young man, who came and went so quietly, who carried my little boys away on his shoulders and sent them back to me happy with a handful of bright, new silver half-dollars. The "knights of the green table" were the aristocracy of the town. They were always the best-dressed men, had full pockets, lived well, were generous, respectful, and kind- hearted. They were in that day much what the stock-broking fraternity was here in San Francisco in the palmy days of the Comstock. The great gambling house of Smith & Barker was the central point of interest. At night, under a glow of tallow candles, fifteen faro tables were surrounded by an eager, restless, reckless crowd. Stakes ran high into the thousands. Fortunes were won or lost on the turning of a card. Great piles of coin and bags of dust lay heaped on every table, and changed hands every minute. Men plunged wildly into every mode of dissipation to drown the homesickness so often gnawing at their hearts. They sang, danced, drank and caroused all night, and worked all day. They were possessed of the demon of recklessness, which always haunted the early mining camps. Blood was often shed, for a continual war raged between the miners and the gamblers. Nearly every man carried in his belt either knife or pistol, and one or the other flashed out on small provocation to do its deadly work.

It was such a circumstance as this which raised the first mob in Nevada City. So far as I ever learned, I was their only victim. One night I was sitting quietly by the kitchen fire, alone. My husband was away at Marysville, attending court. Suddenly I heard low knocks on the boards all round the house. Then I heard from threatening voices the cry, "Burn the house." I looked out of the window and saw a crowd of men at the back of the house. I picked up the candle and went into the dining room. At every window I caught sight of faces pressed against the glass. I hurried to the front, where the knocking was loudest and the voices were most uproarious. Terrified almost to death, I opened the door, just enough to see the host of angry, excited faces and hear the cries, "Search for him" and "No, no, burn him out." I attempted to shut the door, but could not. Some one spoke to me, called himself my friend, and tried to tell me that they meant me no harm. But I could not understand, and answered, "I have no friends; what do you want?" The sheriff, a kindly gentleman, whom I knew well and who lived in my house, tried vainly to calm my fears. He explained that a gambler named Tom Collins had been killed at a card table by one of his associates who lived in our house and that they were searching for him. Finally my old friend, Mr. Nick Turner, came pushing through the crowd and he, with the sheriff, succeeded in allaying my fright and making me understand. I then let them search the house but the man was not there. Had he been caught they would have made short work of him. The next night, or rather in the morning, my husband came home. He had seen the fugitive, who had ridden into Marysville to tell him of the shooting and of my fright. In disguise he had stood in the crowd, not ten feet from me, had watched them search, and heard the raging of the infuriated crowd. He said it was hard work to keep from betraying himself when he saw how I was suffering from terror. His friends had provided a fleet mule, which they had tied somewhere across the ravine, and when the mob dispersed he made fast time out of the camp. Many years afterwards he came to see me and told me that the greatest regret he felt in regard to the affair was that he had not come forward and given himself up and saved me such pain.

The doctors were busy then, for there were hundreds of men sick and dying from cold and exposure. Indeed, every profession found employment, except the clerical, for it was not yet settled enough at the "Coyote" to require the services of a pastor. Every man was too busy thinking of the preservation of his body to think of saving his soul; and the unfortunates who did not succeed in keeping their heads above water were buried "without benefit of the clergy." Like all California mining towns, Nevada City grew up in almost the twinkling of an eye. There were ten thousand men in the Coyote Diggings, and the streets were lined with drinking saloons and gambling tables. Money came in in thousands of dollars from the mines. New parties came pouring into the town from Sacramento and fitted out here for further prospecting in the mountains. The country was full of men crazed on the subject of "deep diggings," and the future seemed to promise a succession of greater good fortune. These were indeed "flush times." We made money fast. In six months we had ten thousand dollars invested in the hotel and store and we owned a stock of goods worth perhaps ten thousand more. The buildings were of the roughest possible description, but they were to Nevada City what the Palace Hotel is to this city today.

There was no place of deposit for money, and the men living in the house dropped into the habit of leaving their dust with me for safe keeping. At times I have had a larger amount of money in my charge than would furnish capital for a country bank. Many a night have I shut my oven door on two milk-pans filled high with bags of gold dust, and I have often slept with my mattress literally lined with the precious metal. At one time I must have had more than two hundred thousand dollars lying unprotected in my bedroom, and it never entered my head that it might be stolen. The house had neither locks nor bolts, but, as there were no thieves, precautions were unnecessary. I had a large, old-fashioned reticule hung behind my kitchen stove, where I put the money I had made by doing little pieces of sewing for the men. In a month or two I had four or five hundred dollars saved and was thinking of lending it, for interest was very high. But one day I missed the bag. Of course there was a general search, and I found, at last, that my youngest son had taken it down, dragged it out into the sand in the street, and was building houses with the coins. He had been there an hour or more, some of the men told me, and no one had thought of stealing even a solitary half-dollar from the little fellow. I loaned the money, but at such an extravagant rate of interest that I might have foreseen that my man must fail and run away, which he finally did. I believe the rate of interest at which I loaned it was ten per cent a month. The only case of theft I can remember to have occurred during the time I lived in Nevada City, was that of a man who appropriated a mule, and he received so aggravated a punishment that I shiver when I recollect that I was an involuntary looker-on. They tied the miserable man to a tree, and lashed his bare back with a leather whip, until he was cut and striped in a hundred places, and the blood ran down from his shoulders to the ground in a perfect stream.

My wardrobe was still a simple one. For several years my best dress was a clean calico. The first installments of genuine finery which came into the interior were crepe shawls and scarfs from the Chinese vessels which came to San Francisco. But the feminine portion of the population was so small that there was no rivalry in dress or fashion, and every man thought every woman in that day a beauty. Even I have had men come forty miles over the mountains, just to look at me, and I never was called a handsome woman, in my best days, even by my most ardent admirers.

View of Nevada City from Prospect Hill, published by Charles W. Mulford in 1850. The arrow identifies Luzena's El Dorado Hotel. David A. Comstock, Gold Diggers and Camp Followers 1845–1851. *See map on page 75 for names of other buildings.*

13 *I called my hotel El Dorado . . .*

THE HARSH WINTER HAD DROPPED A HEAVY LOAD OF RAIN AND SNOW on the Sierra. Using the rainfall at Sacramento as a basis, the precipitation at Nevada City that winter was later estimated at nearly 108 inches, but no one kept an accurate tally. Aaron Sargent, a twenty-three-year-old miner, said that "in March 1850, the snow was ten feet deep on the banks of Deer Creek."[1] As Luzena was trudging through the mud and snow to reach her new home, a record snowpack was accumulating higher in the Sierra, storing up the water the miners would need for the dry season operations in the Coyote Diggings which lacked a year-round supply.

Luzena was inspired to start her boarding house when she saw the sign posted for Womack's Hotel. Two men, Womack and Kenzie, had just opened their hotel in a cloth-covered building on the corner of today's Main and Commercial Streets. Luzena set up her "rival hotel" on the west side of Main Street a little further down the hill, and there were already other boarding houses. Later in May, the going price for boarders at Nick Turner's Nevada Hotel was $25 per week, the same rate Luzena charged. Turner liked to boast that his Nevada was the first wooden-frame hotel in town, measuring 38 by 48 feet, with every piece of wood taken from one pine tree.

A few stores and miscellaneous dwellings rounded out the architectural inventory of the small town that miner Benjamin Avery dubbed "Mushroom City" that spring. "The mines yielded wonderfully," he recalled, and quite naturally people poured in. By August the *Placer Times* reported the population at two thousand, "with four times that number within a circuit of four miles." These numbers tally with Luzena's estimate of ten thousand. Avery called it "a wild, wonderful scene" to see the tents and cabins at night and to hear music and voices echo through the forest of pines.[2]

The El Dorado Hotel made money quickly and Luzena began to diversify. First she took Mason on as a business partner, a clear indication that hers was the leading role in the new enterprise. More boarders came, leading to more construction and the hiring of employees, all proudly recounted by Luzena. In addition, the Wilsons opened a store and stocked it with an estimated $10,000 inventory. Then she established herself as an early California banker, holding gold dust for clients in her primitive vaults—her oven and under her mattress. She even lent money at interest, although she wryly notes that one client skipped town when he could not pay her. Altogether, she had an impressive little business empire.

As Luzena noted, food and supply prices were high but no deterrent to sales. The figures Luzena cited are confirmed by other examples from Aaron Sargent: "fresh beef and pork sold at 80 cents per pound; molasses, $7.50 per gallon; flour at 44 cents; potatoes 75 cents; onions, $1.50; calf boots $20; stout boots from $30 to $40; long handled shovels, $16." Similarly, Benjamin Avery remembered buying $6 whiskey and $8 brandy. Forty-niners frequently remarked on the high cost of living in their letters and diaries. Although the immigrants became accustomed to these prices, such costs would have shocked their friends and family back home. To afford all this, the men had to keep up the constant search for gold.

Miners were finding the "easy" gold in these early days. Avery said the area was known for "pound diggings," meaning a man could find twelve Troy ounces or so per day. The miners patronized the entertainment houses in town for amusement. "Gambling, of course, was common and fatal affrays were frequent," wrote Avery, who later became a newspaperman. Barker's Exchange, which Luzena called "Smith and Barker," was across the street from the El Dorado Hotel. Barker's may have been the place where the gambler Tom Collins was killed. The mob searching for his slayer invaded Luzena's house and frightened her, but she came to no harm. The mining community seemed to tolerate an occasional killing as long as the violence was confined to the gambling dens.

Luzena had good words to say about the gamblers, considering them "generous, respectful and kind-hearted," an assertion which seems questionable given the predatory nature of the profession. She specifically recalled the young Billy Briggs and his playfulness with her two sons. She was not the only one to regard Briggs with affection. When he died in 1889 at age fifty-nine, the *San Francisco Call* newspaper deemed him a man of "singular contrasts" with a reputation for charity, honesty and kindliness who nonetheless profited from the "folly of his fellows." He donated to worthy causes and was generous to friends, especially old pioneers who had fallen on hard times. Many mourners eulogized him, telling

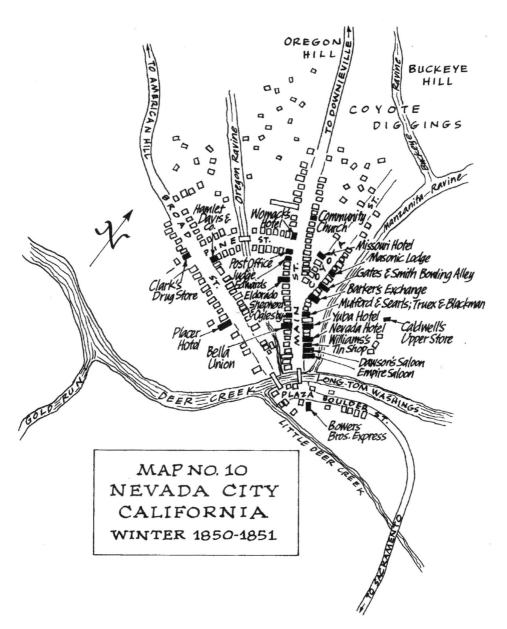

Nevada City Business District in 1850, as drawn by David A. Comstock, Gold Diggers and Camp Followers, 1845–1851.

The San Francisco Call *wrote in gambler Bill Briggs' obituary: "He dealt faro, and considered it a fair battle of luck, but he would not play poker or any other games in which the skill of the player is supposed to outweigh the chances of fortune." A faro player bets against the dealer, who draws two cards from the deck for each turn. The gambler places his bet on the card he thinks will win; if he loses, the dealer, called the banker, collects the bet. Lithograph by Britton & Rey, California State Library.*

of his good deeds in persuading gullible young men to avoid the gaming rooms. Briggs was also mourned by the socially prominent, including Samuel Clemens, a longtime friend from Hannibal College in Missouri who later achieved fame as writer and humorist Mark Twain.[3] In Luzena's view, the gamblers were both the generous aristocrats and the flash point for bloodshed, yet another example of the contradictory nature of the times.

Luzena remarked on the restlessness that afflicted the miners. Sarah Royce lived in a mining camp near Hangtown during the fall of 1849 and also observed the "sounds of discontent and sadness." She named two reasons: First, "The conditions that the men lived in were so bad as to be unhealthy . . . poor diet and hygiene was bound to encourage disease . . . overexertion, changes in lifestyle, and depression led to a lot of sickness." Second, they had to give up the dream of wealth. "These men had come to California to become easily and rapidly rich." In reality, the work was hard, the rewards usually not great, and the expenses very high. For many, all the gold they could find was spent on survival or gambled away. Disillusionment was swallowed daily, but still the feverish dream of "tomorrow's strike" seized their brains. William Pleasants, mining on the Feather River, agreed with this analysis. He said that for every man who found a profitable claim, there were ten more who just scraped by:

> *As a business proposition, mining for gold is most uncertain in its results and demoralizing in its influences, inasmuch as it unfits a man for other more legitimate pursuits. . . . So far as I am concerned, it seems to me that my lack of success in the mines was a blessing in disguise.*

With all the gold around and so many strangers thrown together, it was remarkable that theft was uncommon. Luzena's story of the man whipped for "appropriating a mule" is confirmed in a July 22, 1850 article in the *Sacramento Transcript,* reporting the news in Nevada City:

> *Punishment of criminals is very severe. . . . An individual who had been mining took a notion to a good mule not belonging to him, but he did not travel far before he was overtaken and brought before a jury. . . . He was found guilty of theft, not only of the mule, but also the earnings of the young man who had placed confidence in him, [and who] gave him his bag of gold dust to take out. . . . The verdict of guilty was given . . . and his punishment twenty-five lashes on his bare back, and [he was] compelled to work at $5 per day till the eleven ounces [gold] were returned. I have to write that one cut more was given for interest.*

Punishment for thieves was even harsher in other communities; Hangtown got its name after three were hanged. Nonetheless, Sarah Royce said, ". . . for a while, at least, in those early days, life and property were very safe in the mines; unless indeed you chose to associate with gamblers and desperados, in which case you of course constantly risked your money and your life."

NOTES

1. Aaron Augustus Sargent, *1848–1851: 150 Years Ago,* 6.
2. Wells, Wilson, Rice and Freeman, *History of Nevada County,* 79–80.
3. *San Francisco Call,* April 23, 1889, 2.

14 *Luzena:* NEVADA CITY AND SACRAMENTO
1850–1851

FTER WE HAD BEEN IN THE TOWN OF NEVADA CITY three or four months, the first ball was given. There were twelve ladies present and about three hundred men. The costumes were eccentric, or would be now. At that time it was the prevailing fashion for the gentlemen to attend social gatherings in blue woolen shirts, and with trousers stuffed into boot-tops. Every man was "heeled" with revolver and bowie-knife. My own elaborate toilet for the occasion was a freshly ironed calico and a plaid shawl. The dresses of the other ladies were similar. A few days before the ball, word came into the town that a family of immigrants, including several grown young ladies, had moved into Grass Valley. The news was hailed with rapture by the young men, and two of them, Messrs. Frinx and Blackman, prominent merchants, procured horses and rode over, with testimonials in hand, to engage the presence of the young ladies, if possible, for the forthcoming ball. They were cordially received, and their request gracefully accorded. On the day of the ball, they procured what they could in the form of vehicles, and drove over the mountains to bring back their prizes. It was already dark when they arrived at the little log house, and a knock at the door ushered them into the one room of the residence. The old lady answered their inquiries for the young ladies by saying, "Not much. If your ball had been in the daytime, and the gals 'ud by home by dark, I wouldn't mind; but my gals don't go traipsing 'round in the night with no young men. No siree."

There was nothing left for the discomfited beaux but to come back alone. When they returned, they gave us a mournful description of their wild-goose chase. They told us how, as they stepped into the room, the clothing on two beds gave a sudden jerk and exposed the symmetry of two pairs of feet. They were at first mystified by the strange sight, but afterwards concluded that these were the dainty pedal extremities of their missing inamoratas. However, the ball went on, notwithstanding the lessening in number of the expected ladies. A number of the men tied handkerchiefs around their arms and airily assumed the character of ball-room belles. Every lady was overwhelmed with attentions, and there was probably more enjoyment that night, on the rough pine floor and under the flickering gleam of tallow candles, than one often finds in our society drawing-rooms, where the rich silks trail over velvet carpets, where the air is heavy with the perfume of exotics, and where night is turned into a brighter day under the glare of countless gas-jets.

We had lived eighteen months in Nevada City when fire cut us adrift again, as water had done in Sacramento. Some careless hand had set fire to a pile of pine shavings lying at the side of a house in course of construction, and while we slept, unconscious of danger, the flames caught and spread, and in a short half hour the whole town was in a blaze. We were roused from sleep by the cry of "Fire, fire" and the clang of bells. Snatching each a garment, we hurried out through blinding smoke and darting flames, not daring even to make an effort to collect our effects. There were no means for stopping such a conflagration. Bells clanged and gongs sounded, but all to no purpose save to wake the sleeping people, for neither engines nor firemen were at hand. So we stood with bated breath, and watched the fiery monster crush in his great red jaws the homes we had toiled to build. The tinder-like pine houses ignited with a spark, and the fire raged and roared over the fated town. The red glare fell far back into the pine woods and lighted them like day; it wrapped the moving human creatures in the fiendish glow, and cast their giant shadows far along the ground. The fire howled and moaned like a giant in an agony of pain, and buildings crashed and fell as if he were striking them down in his writhings. When the slow dawn broke, and the sun came riding up so calm and smiling, he looked down upon a smouldering bed of ashes; and in place of the cheerful, happy faces, which were wont to greet his appearance in the busy rushing town of yesterday his beams lighted sad countenances, reflecting the utter ruin of their fortunes. The eight thousand inhabitants were homeless, for in the principal part of the town every house was swept away; and most of them were penniless as well as homeless. Like ourselves most of them had invested their money in buildings and goods, and scarcely anything was saved. The remnant of our fortune consisted of five hundred dollars, which my husband had in his pockets and had neglected to put away, and with that sum we were to start again. For months my health had been failing, and when this blow came in the shape of the fire, my strength failed and I fell sick. Some generous man offered us the shelter of his cabin in the edge of the woods. For weeks I was a prisoner there, bound in the fetters of fever. When, at last, my returning health and strength permitted it, we moved from Nevada City nearer to the valley.

The mines around Nevada City were wonderfully rich. Miles and miles of flume carried the water from mine to mine, to flow on through more miles of sluice-boxes. Claims were staked off in every ravine for hangers about the city. Men dug for gold in the very streets of the town and under the very foundations of the houses. Not infrequently the digging of a well would develop a rich claim and make the owner rich in a few weeks. After the fire we let our city lot go for a few dollars and the man who bought it took thirty thousand dollars out of the gravel part of it, which sloped down to the ravine. The streams ran muddy with the tailings from the diggings. Wherever pick and shovel disturbed and water washed the soil, a color could be found. Many men made fortunes, for thousands of dollars were taken out in a single day. The fever and uncertainty of mining made the people grow old and haggard. They might dig, dig, dig, fruitlessly for days, making scarcely enough to keep body and soul together, and then disheartened, sell the worthless claim for enough provisions to last till they struck another camp. Perhaps the first day's work on the old claim by the new owner would yield hundreds of dollars. Not a half block from my house, a young man took out sixteen thousand dollars, and then gave his claim to me. I had no way to work it, and my husband was opposed to mining on general principles, so I sold the property for a hundred dollars. The man who bought it took out of it, before we left the town, ten thousand dollars.

Nevada City sprung, Phoenix like, from its ashes and grew up a more substantial and permanent town and with more consideration for appearances. The streets straightened themselves, the houses, like well-drilled soldiers, formed naturally into line. The little city was more rushing and prosperous than ever. The green valleys, however, seemed to offer us a pleasanter home, so we adhered to our plan of removal, and bade a rather sad farewell to the bright, spicy little snow-bound town where we had found so many friends.

The road we followed back to Sacramento had greatly changed since we had traveled over it eighteen months before. Where we had climbed up and down steep mountains, and cut down obstacles in our path, we now rose and descended by easy grades. The woods, which had then closed around dark and thick, had been charred or burned away, and the giant arms, scorched and blackened, pointed out the new way. Substantial bridges spanned the streams.

Every turn brought us face to face with wagons loaded high with building materials and supplies for the city of the mountains. Instead of the twelve dragging days we spent in our first trip over this route, the journey was performed in two. Instead of sleeping in discomfort on the cold, wet ground, we enjoyed the hospitality of a comfortable house, the property of Mr. James Anthony.

This hotel, at the crossing of Bear River was, for the times, something remarkable. There for the first time in California I saw papered and painted walls. The floors were covered with China matting, and the beds rejoiced in sheets and pillowcases. The carpeting was a real luxury, and I remember thinking if I could get a house carpeted with that beautiful covering I should scarcely care for anything else, for relief from the drudgery of scrubbing floors seemed the one thing worth living for. It was a bachelor establishment, but, strange to say, was scrupulously clean and well conducted. Had he known it, the genial proprietor might have resented my husband's speech to me, "Don't you think you had better go out and see if supper is all right?"

As we came down from the mountains we found the country stirred up with "squatter" troubles, rumors of which had reached us in Nevada. As we neared Sacramento we found ourselves almost in the midst of them. The trouble originated through the conflicting claims of the buyers and settlers. Almost all the land, from some distance below Sacramento far up into the Shasta region, was claimed by Sutter under a Spanish grant; and the towns of Sacramento, Brighton, Marysville, Coloma, and others, and the lands surrounding them, were sold by Sutter, or his representatives, under the grant title. Numbers of the newcomers resented this claim and pre-empted land under the United States laws. Naturally there arose between the rival claimants a war which was often a bloody one. The first serious outbreak to occur was "the squatter riot of '51." I believe the first real trouble took place near Sacramento, in the endeavor of the people on the grant side of the faction to dispossess the Madden brothers, Jerome and Thomas. The settlers gathered in a body, reinstated them, and paraded through the streets of Sacramento. The city turned out in force, headed by the sheriff, mayor and other officials in opposition, and a fight took place in which Bigelow, the mayor, Woodland, the assessor, and Maloney, the captain of the settlers were killed and several on both sides wounded.

There were many episodes at that time that would be more thrilling than romance. One of the most talked of incidents was the killing of Sheriff McKenna at the house of William Allan, near Brighton. Allan, who was supposed to be in league with the squatters, had been heard to make sympathizing remarks to and about them, and by his course had incurred the wrath of the officials. A posse, headed by the sheriff returning from the funeral of the murdered mayor and assessor, rode out to arrest the suspected man. They knocked at the door, and were told that Mrs. Allan was very sick, perhaps dying, and were requested to retire. Allan promised to come to Sacramento and give himself up in the morning. But during the discussion some one fired a pistol, whether intentionally or not was never known; and the guard, thinking someone was resisting the sheriff, broke open the doors and fired upon the occupants of the room, killing Allan's son and wounding the old man himself in two places. A shot, inflicted by McKenna, wounded him in the right arm as he stood with revolver drawn. The weapon fell, but the determined old man grasped it with his left hand and fired the shot which killed the officer. When their leader fell, the posse withdrew to a distance, but, ascertaining his fate, returned in hot haste to the house. I was told by an eye-witness that, as they looked through the open door, they saw dead upon the bed the poor mother, her features drawn and distorted by the fright which had hastened her approaching end. Bending over her, apparently brokenhearted, was the daughter, with pale face and horror-stricken eyes, and dead at her feet, in a pool of blood lay the son. The sight of so much misery seemed to touch no tender cord in the bosoms of the enraged men and they searched with intent eyes and strained ears for a sound which might tell of their victim's hiding-place; but he baffled pursuit. They rode up and down the river for several miles, searched out-houses, and beat the bushes but failed to find him. It was not until years after that I heard the almost miraculous story of his preservation. He crept to the river, and hung to the willows in the water, with his face raised only to admit his breathing, while the pursuers passed and repassed at the distance of a few feet. At last when silence told of their withdrawal, he swam the river and sought shelter in a neighboring barn. It was not till five days after that he crept unobserved into Coloma, and obtained medical attendance for his wounds, which the hot weather had aggravated into a death-like torture. His friends came to his assistance and he was safely hidden from pursuit and helped out of the State, and it was many years before he dared openly to show himself in California. His life, however, ended peacefully a few years ago in the calm and seclusion of Lake County.

Miners Dancing in a Saloon: *Artist unknown. Eleanor McClatchy Collection, Sacramento Archives and Museum Collection Center.*

15 *A smouldering bed of ashes . . .*

THE NEVADA CITY MINERS ENJOYED DANCING and the ball that Luzena described must have been a social highlight. Given the shortage of ladies, it was common for the men to "assume the character of ballroom belles," as Luzena delicately put it. Usually the men who obligingly took the female role declared their identity by a scrap of cloth tied around an arm or adopted some other simple device. "One method for temporarily canceling manhood was a strategically tacked patch of calico upon the "ladies'" trousers."[1] The two disappointed gentlemen who failed to procure the hands of the Grass Valley damsels for the ball were mostly likely O. P. Blackman and Edward H. Truex, not Blackman and Frinx, as Luzena wrote. These two eligible bachelors were partners in a general merchandise store in town. Blackman is generally credited with suggesting the name "Nevada," meaning "snowy" in Spanish, for the town. On Christmas night, another ball was given by Nick Turner, the well-liked proprietor of the Nevada Hotel; admission was $10.[2]

As 1850 came to an end, the merchants began to stockpile goods in anticipation of another brutal winter. But the rainfall was exceptionally light that season. The lack of water was a serious blow to the miners who needed a steady supply for their dams and sluices. Some people left town and the merchants were left with large inventories. But at the beginning of 1851 things began to look better. Mining resumed and business picked up. Then disaster struck in the early hours of March 12.

Some believed the fire was deliberately set, the revenge of a suspected thief who had been whipped and driven out of town the day before. The culprit was never found, however. Flames first broke out at about one o'clock in the morning at Gates and Smith's bowling ball alley and quickly spread throughout the business section. Some tall pines stood amid the buildings and "these trees," miner Aaron Sargent said, "extremely pitchy, caught the flames as they writhed round their stems, and shot them hundreds of feet into the air, where they danced and quivered like malicious spirits over the scene of a burning world." There was no water to stop the fire, so the men tore down buildings in its path to contain the flames. When the sun came up, all that was left of Nevada City was charred remnants and ashes. Losses were estimated at more than half a million dollars in property and merchandise, with 150 buildings destroyed. The *Sacramento Transcript* put the Wilson's losses at $4,000, but doubtless they reckoned the amount many times higher.

Luzena was most discouraged by the loss of her business and a fever overtook her for a time. Medical care in the mines was a rather hit-and-miss affair. According to Sargent, "The only kinds of medicines in the pharmacopeia of the physicians in those days were calomel, laudanum and opium, which were administered for all diseases and wounds, with little respect for the symptoms." Perhaps Luzena sought advice from Dr. Lark, whose Drug and Medicine Store was also consumed by the fire. The Wilsons decided not to participate in the

A lettersheet depicts the burning of Nevada City. Luzena's El Dorado Hotel was located in the middle of this inferno. Eleanor McClatchy Collection, Sacramento Archives and Museum Collection Center.

Nevada City's quick recovery is documented in an 1858 daguerreotype. Carl Mautz Collection.

rebuilding of Nevada City, but packed up to return to Sacramento. Luzena said they lived in Nevada City for eighteen months, but actually their stay lasted little more than one year.

They sold their property to a miner, Luzena said, but probably no legal papers ever changed hands. Few land transactions were recorded then. Property was claimed by the first occupying settler, and when the owner moved he sold the land without formality. This is probably how the Wilsons bought and sold their parcels, both of which yielded gold after passing out of their hands. Since Mason was "opposed to mining on general principles," Luzena had to sell the claim she had received as a gift. Her tone seems somewhat regretful when she remembers, "I had no way to work it;" perhaps her opinion of mining differed from that of her husband. When her buyer proceeded to get $10,000 in gold from the claim, Luzena and Mason may well have had words! One wonders when Mason's opposition to gold mining developed because he certainly had gold fever when he left Missouri.

Luzena met some intriguing people during her stay in the mountains and some went on to notable careers. The gambler, Billy Briggs, achieved some notoriety as a colorful character in San Francisco. At the Bear River crossing, Mason and Luzena enjoyed the hospitality of hotelier James Anthony. Mason expressed skepticism about the meals at this bachelor's table and Luzena seemed amused at his concern; maybe she took it as a compliment to her own skills and standards. This man pursuing business in Placer County probably was the same James Anthony who later owned and published the *Sacramento Union*. According to Mark Twain, Anthony and his business associates were the "best men to ever own a newspaper."[3] Anthony would do battle with the Central Pacific Railroad in the 1860s to combat what he saw as the malignant influence of the railroad.

Aaron Augustus Sargent, a miner and another Nevada City memorist, became prominent in law, journalism, and finally, politics. He was elected as a Republican to the U.S. Congress three times, and in 1873 became a U.S. Senator. In 1878 he introduced a resolution to grant women the right to vote, a bill later known as the Susan B. Anthony Amendment. It was her original language in his bill that finally became the Nineteenth Amendment to the U.S. Constitution in 1920. His wife, Ellen Clark Sargent, was an early advocate of women's rights and clearly a strong influence on him as he held to his unpopular stance. When he spoke on the Senate floor regarding the issue, some of his colleagues considered him deranged.[4] The Wilsons' path would cross Mr. Sargent's again in later years. As their congressman in 1861, he helped secure an appointment to the U.S. Naval Academy for Luzena's son Thomas.

Sacramento 1850

"Squatter troubles" were stirring in the valley when the Wilsons moved back to Sacramento. Luzena had heard tales of the conflicts while in Nevada City, and correctly identified the root of the disputes. The landholders had bought their property from Captain John A. Sutter who held title under a Mexican land grant. The treaty which ended the Mexican–American War and made California a U.S. territory, specified that the United States would honor the Mexican land titles. However, many immigrants refused to recognize the validity of grants such as Sutter's, and were angered that some of the best properties were already taken. They believed any vacant land was fair game and could be claimed by a newcomer who was willing to settle the acreage. This was the case in Oregon where "squatter sovereignty, free and untrammelled" ruled, as well as in the Middle West.[5] In 1849 most new arrivals in California went straight to the gold fields; few people desiring land stayed long in Sacramento. But in 1850 squatter leaders expected a new wave of immigrants to swell their ranks, and the opposition intensified against landholders such as Sam Brannan and Captain Sutter.

In August 1850, not 1851 as Luzena said, the situation came to a head, following a steady buildup of hostilities both in and out of court. John Madden (not the brothers Jerome and Thomas Madden that Luzena named) had been squatting on a lot at the corner of Second and N Streets. Unhappy with the court decision that had evicted him, he occupied it again on August 14. A group of nearly forty armed men launched a street demonstration in support of Madden's cause. Led by William Malony, they marched through the city, evidently intent on freeing some colleagues who had been jailed the day before. Seeing the excitement, a large crowd of unarmed citizens followed the marchers, jeering at them and generally enjoying a lark. The authorities were completely unprepared for any confrontation. Mayor Hardin Bigelow rode through the streets urging the group of laughing followers to help him stop this nonsense. Sheriff Joseph McKinney,

The Illustrated Placer Times and Transcript *portrayed the dramatic events of the Squatter Riot of 1850 in an 1852 retrospective edition. Eleanor McClatchy Collection, Sacramento Archives and Museum Collection Center.*

NOTICE
TO
IMMIGRANTS!!

As there are in our City a number of men with remarkable principles, who go among those who have newly arrived and offer to sell or lease to them the *Public Land* in and about this place, thus imposing upon the unsuspecting. The latter are hereby notified that the vacant land in Sacramento City and vicinity, is open for *ALL*, free of charge ; but, they can make either of the following gentlemen a present of a few thousand dollars, if they have it to spare. Such favors are eagerly sought and ex-ultingly received by them. In fact, some of them are so solicitous in this matter, that, if they are not given *something*, they will *almost not like it*, and even threaten to *sue* people who will not contribute to their support. Those who have made themselves the most notorious, are

Barton Lee,	Prettyman, Barroll & Co.,	Warbass & Co.,
Burnett & Rogers,	A. M. Winn	J. Sherwood,
Hardin Bigelow,	S. Brannan,	James Queen,
Pearson & Baker,	Hensley, Merrill & King,	Dr. W. G. Deal,
Thomas M'Dowell,	Conn. Mining and Trading Co.,	Eugene F. Gillespie,
R. J. Watson,	Paul, White & Co.,	T. L. Chapman,
J. S. Hambleton,	W. M. Carpenter,	Dewey & Smith,
Starr, Bensley & Co.,	R. Gelston,	E. L. Brown,
	John S. Fowler.	

Sacramento City, June 14, 1850.

"Sacramento Transcript" Print.

By order of the Settlers' Association.

Notice to Immigrants, Eleanor McClatchy Collection, Sacramento Archives and Museum Collection Center.

age twenty-one, rode alongside the Mayor as they moved through the crowd toward the squatters. Suddenly, the squatters looked around and saw the pursuing authorities. Bigelow shouted an order to disperse and the squatters responded with gunfire. The Mayor was hit several times and fell, seriously injured; John Woodland, the city assessor, was killed instantly. The Sheriff and some of the Mayor's supporters returned fire. Malony was shot dead trying to escape and two other squatters also died. There were injuries on both sides. The crowd melted away rapidly and the streets were soon quiet.

Rumors immediately began to swirl and people wondered if and when the squatters would strike again. The next day, Sheriff McKinney rode with an armed posse out to Brighton, located near where Folsom Boulevard now meets Highway 50. He had arrest warrants for some squatters who had been seen drinking in a bar owned by James (not William) Allen, also known as "Old Man Allen" or

"Horse Allen." Luzena relayed the scene as an eyewitness told it to her and the story seems reasonably accurate when compared to other accounts. In the darkness it was hard to be sure of the order of events, but the sheriff was immediately gunned down after he demanded Allen's surrender. The sheriff's party peppered the house with bullets, killing two and wounding others. Allen escaped by hiding in the river as Luzena heard. He went back to Missouri for several years, but returned to California in the 1860s. He was never prosecuted for the death of the Sheriff, nor were any of the other squatters involved in the earlier killings.

The squatters lost considerable public support in the wake of these events. Clearly they had fired first and the townspeople were frightened at the potential for further lawlessness. It would take many years and endless litigation before all the Mexican land grant disputes were resolved, but this first riot seemed to slow the squatters' momentum.

To add to Sacramento's woe in 1850, there had been a second flood in March, and a fire in April destroyed at least eight downtown buildings. In August and September, a string of banking houses shut down and the resulting financial panic rippled throughout the city. Then a cholera epidemic broke out in October, just days after the news of California's admission to the Union reached the city. For several weeks, death was a frequent visitor as the infection spread quickly and claimed many lives. Still, the gold from the mines kept coming and the city kept growing, with youthful resilience and heady abandon. The Wilsons returned to a city that had endured a lot.

NOTES

1. Jo Ann Levy, *They Saw the Elephant,* 182.
2. David Allen Comstock, *Gold Diggers and Camp Followers,* 342.
3. John Healey, ed., *Editors West,* 22.
4. Heather Macdonald., undated article, *Union.*
5. Josiah Royce, "The Squatter Riot of '50 in Sacramento," *Overland Monthly,* 228.

16 *Luzena:* SACRAMENTO AND VACA VALLEY
1851

WHEN WE REACHED SACRAMENTO AGAIN WE BECAME UNDECIDED whether to go on toward the bay or to remain there. In the meantime we took possession of a deserted hotel which stood on K Street. This hotel was tenanted only by rats that galloped madly over the floor and made journeys from room to room through openings they had gnawed in the panels. They seemed to have no apprehension of human beings and came and went as fearlessly as if we had not been there. At that time Sacramento was infested with the horrible creatures. They swarmed from the vessels lying at the wharves into the town and grew into a thriving colony which neither flood nor fire could subdue. In the flood of '49 I had seen dozens of them collected upon every floating stick, or box, or barrel, and had seen men push them off into the water and watch them scramble back to another resting-place. Every rope and board would be alive with them. They ran backward and forward across the chains that held the vessels to the piers. All of them seemed to have survived the second flood as well, and when we spent the first night in that deserted house it seemed that all their descendants had gathered there to hold high carnival. As it grew dark they came out by scores, and my husband threw a little barley on the ground in the back yard to see how many would collect there. It was not many minutes till the yard was covered with rats; they seemed piled three deep in their ravenous hunger for the grain; when my husband fired into them with a shot-gun, he killed thirty-two. A second shot killed twelve, and I believe if he had continued his curious sport he might have killed hundreds. From every corner they glared at us with their round, bright eyes. They snapped at our heels as we passed. They bit at each other, and gnawed the legs of chairs where we sat. At night I put the bedding upon the tables, lest in our sleep the fierce creatures would be tempted to make their raids upon our bodies. I listened with perfect horror to their savage wrangling over bits of discarded food which had been left lying about. Even rat-terriers and ferocious cats came off second best in their encounters with the pests.

Sacramento had very greatly changed since our departure after the flood of '49. We had left the town covered with slime and mud; with dirty canvases clinging to broken poles; with festering carcasses in the streets; with drift-wood caught at every obstructing point; with yawning mudholes at every corner; with floundering teams and miring wagons everywhere to be seen. We had left it full of men with broken fortunes, with long faces and empty pockets. A second flood had come and gone and the city, newly risen from the waters, was built up along broad, graded streets with large airy, well-built houses. Brick and mortar had taken the place of canvas and shakes. Sidewalks gave the pedestrian security against dust and mud. Well-stocked stores of dry goods, groceries, and hardware had taken the place of the redwood board over the barrel-head. An enterprising daguerreotypist had set up his sign in the city, and was doing a rushing business at thirty dollars a picture. The banking house of Page & Bacon was one of the solid institutions of the time. Adams Express transported dust and valuables. The pony express thundered into Sacramento every day, connecting the East with the West. The overland stage drew up with a flourish, and emptied its weight of mails and freight of passengers into the eager hands of the waiting Californians. Other lines of stages ran in all direction to the mines, and steamers came up from San Francisco. The town was full of people and full of money. The "Golden Eagle" still nods in sleepy indolence on the same spot on K street where it then stood, wide awake and bustling, with "Mine host" Callahan smiling pleasantly and accommodatingly on his guests. The little fish of the puddle waked up to the sense that they were quite grown up and required amusement. The city boasted a theatre; and stars in eclipse or waiting for a first bright dawning walked the boards in proud consciousness of their unappreciated worth. The first play I saw there was "Julius Caesar." In the intervals of the tragedy we were regaled with the songs of Charles Vivian. When he came back again, fifteen years later, he revived his songs of '49 *and the great big yellow lumps of gold* and the pioneer airs, *Wapping Old Stairs,* and *The Blue-tailed Fly.*

On the day of a bull fight, or a mustang race, the sporting population turned out en masse, and the victory or defeat of Chiquita or Rag-tailed Billy, made their respective owners rich or poor, for no man ever hesitated to bet his bottom dollar on his own horse. I have seen them come home sometimes bootless, coatless, hatless, from the track, having parted with those articles as the exigencies of the race demanded, and when they handed over their red sashes and silver-plated, chain-decked spurs, the struggle was like the severing of soul and body. Sometimes the losing turfman shot his defeated horse, as a sort of sedative to his irritated feelings. The streets were lined with gambling houses and whisky shops. Every second door on J Street led to a faro table and a bar, and every place was thronged with customers. Sacramento was filled with desperadoes, and almost every twenty-four hours witnessed at least one murder. So long as the gamblers confined their murderous attack among their own kind, no one paid much attention to their sport, but when their blows fell on an outsider with fatal result, vengeance was swift and sure, for the population took the matter into their own hands in defiance of law. The second day after we had arrived such an episode occurred.

A young man walking down the street was attracted by a street brawl among the gamblers, an occurrence so frequent that had it not been for the manifest injustice of one man being assailed by two, it would have passed unnoticed. As it was, he generously interfered, separated the combatants and released the weaker party. Enraged at the uncalled for obtrusion, one of the young ruffians fired upon the intruder, inflicting a mortal wound. Scarcely was the deed committed before the gathering crowd, mad with rage, demanded the murderer's life. The officers whirled away the malefactor, and for lack of another stronghold, confined him in the basement of a brick building of private ownership, pending trial. But as the morning wore on, the fury of the populace grew hotter, and their always existing hatred of the gamblers grew into an ungovernable passion at the one against whom they had a clue. They refused to listen to the advocates of the law. The mob were quick about it. They broke open the improvised jail and dragged the criminal from his prison.

It must have been two o'clock at night when I was startled by the tramp of feet passing by the door. I ran to look and the glimmer of the torches carried by the muttering men revealed in their midst the figure of the murderer. He seemed frozen with terror, his knees knocked together, and his legs refused to support him. He was carried by the men on either side of him. His eyes were starting from their sockets, his face was ghastly, his lips were livid, and his hair stood on end. He seemed not to see the mob about him, who cried, "hang him, hang him," and his fixed eyes dilated with fear at the phantom of death he saw before him. I had not heard the story of the shooting, so I was in ignorance concerning the meaning of the crowd, or what was the fault of the miserable wretch. After they had passed by I ran to the corner, half a block distant, to see where they carried him. As I reached the spot, I saw a black object shoot up into the air above the heads of the swaying mob and dangle from the limb of a great sycamore tree which stood in the street. It writhed and trembled for an instant and was still, and the silence of satisfied revenge settled down over the dispersing crowd. When daylight broke the summer wind swayed to and fro in the warm morning air all that was mortal of the murderer, but not a whisper told whose hands had executed the fearful vengeance. His friends came with the early light to remove the body. He was buried on the following day, and by some strange fatality, the same bright sun shone on the newly made graves, where the murderer and his victim lay sleeping side by side.

We lingered a month or more in Sacramento, undecided what to do, but finally our interest was again strongly attracted to the valley, and, our tastes and former habits being somewhat agricultural, we determined to move on. The tules barred our direct way, stretching in a broad water covered sheet from the Sacramento River ten miles in to land. We could not swim our teams across, as I have known Jerome Davis and his fellow stock-traders to swim their bands of cattle and wire mustangs, so we drove up the river to the ferry, now known as Knight's Landing, and there we crossed over in a flat bottomed ferry-boat.

The plain from the river bank to the mountains was a sheet of waving grass and bright-hued wild flowers, trackless and unenclosed. The fresh spring breezes fanned our faces and invigorated our bodies; the calmness and silence of the wide prairie soothed us like a sweet dream. We journeyed on to the foothills, passing for miles through wild oats which rose to the heads of our mules. Antelopes and elks stopped on every knoll, and, surveying us with startled eyes and uplifted heads, wheeled and galloped out of sight. After four or five days of easy traveling, we pitched our camp over the first range of low outlying foothills at the foot of a spur of the Coast Range.

Our location was close by a tiny spring-fed stream, near the most frequented route from the upper country to Benicia. The shade of a wide-spreading oak afforded us a pleasant shelter from the sunshine, and at night we slept in a tent improvised from the boughs and canvas cover of our wagon. We were fascinated by the beauty of the little valley which already bore the name of Vaca from the

Spanish owner of the grant within the limits of which it lay. The green hills smiled down on us through their sheeny veil of grass. The great oak trees, tall and stately, bent down their friendly arms as if to embrace us; the nodding oats sang a song of peace and plenty to the music of the soft wind; the inquisitive wild flowers, peeping up with round, wide opened eyes from the edge of every foot-path bade us stay. We made up our minds if possible, to buy land and settle.

We were again almost penniless, and we felt that we must get to work and begin to lay by something.

It was early spring time, and the wild oats, growing all about us in such rank profusion, seemed to say, "Here is food and drink and clothing." Hay was selling in San Francisco at a hundred and fifty dollars a ton, so my husband, leaving me to my own resources, set hard at work cutting and making hay; and I , as before, set up my stove and camp kettle and hung out my sign, printed with a charred fire-brand on a piece of board, WILSON'S HOTEL. The accommodations were, perhaps, scanty, but were hailed with delight by the traveling public, which had heretofore lunched or dined on horseback at full gallop, or lain down supperless to sleep under the wide arch of heaven. The boards from the wagon bed made my table, handy stumps and logs made comfortable chairs, and the guest tethered his horse at the distance of a few yards and retired to the other side of the hay-stack to sleep. The next morning he paid me a dollar for his bed and another for his breakfast, touched his sombrero, and with a kind "good morning," spurred his horse and rode away, feeling he had not paid too dearly for his entertainment. My husband's ready rifle supplied the table with roast and steak of antelope and elk from the herds which grazed about us, and the hotel under the oak tree prospered.

There we lived for the whole summer, six months or more without other shelter than the canvas wagon-cover at night and the roof of green leaves by day. Housekeeping was not difficult then, no fussing with servants or house-cleaning, no windows to wash or carpets to take up. I swept away the dirt with a broom of willow switches, and the drawing room where I received my company was "all out doors." When the dust grew inconvenient under foot, we moved the cook stove and table around to the other side of the tree and began over again. A row of nails driven close in the tree trunk held my array of culinary utensils and the polished tin cups which daily graced my table, and a shelf held the bright tin plates from which we ate. No crystal or French decorated egg-shell china added care to my labors. Notwithstanding the lack of modern appliances and conveniences, my hotel had the reputation of being the best on the route from Sacramento to Benicia. The men who came and went up and down the country, and ate frequently at my table, used often to compliment me upon the good cheer which they always found provided, and by pleasing contrast, told stories of the meals they sometimes got at other places. I remember one morning having eight or ten at breakfast, and they vied with each other in relating tales of the poor breakfasts they had eaten. But the palm was carried off by Mr. Thad. Hoppin, who in his slow way, said, "Well, the worst meal I ever ate they gave me yesterday down at Allford's. All they had was clabber milk and seed cucumbers."

My nearest American neighbors were Mr. John Wolfskill, and Mr. and Mrs. Mat. Wolfskill, who lived twelve miles away, on the banks of Putah Creek. After I had been about six months in Vaca Valley, I concluded to ride over and get acquainted. So one morning bright and early, after the breakfast was over, the dishes washed, and the housework finished, I saddled my horse with my husband's saddle (a side-saddle was unknown in those parts), packed a lunch, took a bottle of water, tied my two boys on behind me with a stout rope and started off. I did not know the exact spot where my neighbors lived, but felt sure of finding them without trouble, as I had only to ride on across the plain until I struck the first stream, and follow it down. There were no roads, so I could select my path as I pleased, taking care only to avoid as much as possible the bands of Spanish cattle which covered the whole country; they were dangerous to encounter, even mounted, and to any one on foot they were certain death. We were riding rapidly through the scattered herds, when a sudden gust of wind took away the hat of one of the children, and as a hat was something precious and not easily procured at that time, we must stop and get it. I should hardly have been able to descend and remount without attracting the notice of the cattle by the fluttering of my dress, and then a stampede would inevitably have followed; so I constructed a stirrup of handkerchiefs; then my little boy clambered down and climbed up again, in the face of the tossing heads, red eyes and spreading horns all about us.

At ten o'clock we arrived at a house thatched with tule, and, seeing a man sitting near it we stopped to ask, "Does Mr. Wolfskill live here?" "My name's Wolfskill," was the reply, "but there ain't no mister to it."

I began to introduce myself, when he cut short my speech with, "Git down, git down. I know you. I got a drink at your well yesterday. Git down."

It was not a ceremonious greeting, but it was intended to be a cordial one, and the entire visit proved to be very satisfactory. Mrs. Wolfskill, good woman, was as delighted to find an English-speaking neighbor as I was myself and gave me a hearty welcome. That day saw the commencement of a real friendship between us, which ended only with her death; and thereafter, at short intervals, we rode across the plain to exchange friendly visits, until every vaquero on the grant knew us, and saluted us as we passed with a polite, *"Buenas Dias, senora."* The Los Putos grant, belonging to the Wolfskills, comprised fifty thousand acres of some of the best land in what is now Solano County. But these good people, who were then the possessors of leagues of land and thousands of Spanish cattle, lived in that little tule house with a dirt floor for years. Their children, still living at the same spot, in a great southern-looking, veranda-shaded, cool, stone house, surrounded with orange groves and fig orchards, are the happy possessors of the finest ranches in the country.

In this 1852 daguerreotype of the Adams Express Company, the men managed to stand still for the picture, but the horse and rider at left did not. Of special interest are the crude boardwalks, which afforded pedestrians some escape from the dust and mud of the streets. Eleanor McClatchy Collection, Sacramento Archives and Museum Collection Center.

17 *We determined to move on . . .*

L UZENA'S DESCRIPTION OF THE DREADFUL SWARMS OF RATS was accurate; they were truly a plague. Rats first arrived on the ships and could be seen boldly running on the lines and rigging all over the wharf. During the January 1850 flood they were clinging to anything that floated. Frank Marryat wrote: "These animals come out after dark in strong gangs, as if the town belonged to them, and attack anything that may happen to have been left on the wharf during the night; being very numerous, the destruction they cause to the merchandise is a serious loss."[1] Carl Meyer took it upon himself to conduct a census of their population; in a ten block square he tallied 30,600 rats. It is unlikely the rats stood still for the counting, but surely he saw a lot of them!

Impressive new buildings went up all around town to accommodate booming businesses. The San Francisco banking house of Page and Bacon, remembered by Luzena, set up a Sacramento branch on J Street and proudly advertised its connections to prominent Eastern banks. It went out of business in 1855 when panicky depositors withdrew more funds than the bank and its branches had available. Adams and Company, which provided banking and express services and carried gold dust safely back east, also went out of business in 1855, creating chaos on both coasts. Adams built the first granite building in Sacramento; an early admirer pronounced the three-story structure "perfect in all its parts."[2] The city directory of 1851 lists three daguerreans, four separate Masonic Lodges, and at least three theaters among the business and professional services available. D. E. Callahan, remembered by Luzena as "mine host" of the Golden Eagle, continued to operate a hotel on K Street so she was able to visit at least one old friend in the sea of new arrivals.

Although Luzena's memory seems to be generally reliable, there are a few discrepancies in her story. For instance, she recalls attending a performance of

Julius Caesar and enjoying the songs of Mr. Charles Vivian during the intermission. Luzena may have been mistaken about the play she saw. The Tehama Theater was doing Shakespeare while she was in Sacramento City, but *Julius Caesar* was not listed in the newspaper advertisements at the time. Charles Vivian was born in England in 1846 and did not arrive in America until he was twenty-one, so it was impossible for Luzena to have seen him. Mr. Vivian appeared in Vacaville in 1874, however, and may have found Luzena among his loyal fans. He was an enormously popular singer and comic actor in his day. He toured extensively and thoroughly enjoyed the colorful life of a traveling artist as a devotee of wine, women and song. His memory is kept alive today by the benevolent society he founded: The Order of Elks.

Luzena recalled in vivid detail the lynching she witnessed and her account matches the cautionary tale of Frederick J. Roe, age twenty, a professional gambler from England who was hung in Sacramento after he shot Charles Myers, a wheelwright. The gathering crowd elected a citizen committee on the spot to investigate; their report summarized the facts:

> *That at about two o'clock, P.M. this day, Frederic Rowe [sic] and some other person, whose name is unknown, were engaged in an altercation which originated at a gambling table in the Mansion House; and that after said parties had proceeded into the street, and were there fighting, Charles Myers, who was passing on the street, interfered, with words, by requesting them to desist fighting or to "show fair play"—that immediately thereafter said F. Rowe called out, 'What the devil have you to say,' and then drew his pistol and without further provocation shot said Charles Myers through the head.[3]*

After four hours of intense deliberation under the eyes of a restless mob of citizens who were calling for Roe to be hung, the impromptu jury found him guilty. The crowd attacked the jail with a battering ram, dragged Roe out, and hung him from an oak tree near Sixth and K Streets around ten p.m. As many as 5,000 people may have witnessed this, the city's first lynching. The headline in the *Sacramento Transcript* was triumphant: "Immense Excitement! Lynch Law at Last!!" For many days the newspaper published every available detail of the vigilante action.

Mr. Roe was hung while his victim was still alive, contrary to Luzena's account; Charles Myers lingered for two days before dying of his wounds. At the coroner's inquest into Myers' death, a slightly different version of the shooting was told. Eyewitness William Armstrong saw the fight begin on the street, and saw Myers

CHARLES
VIVIAN!

THE MOST SUCCESSFUL

Comic Vocalist!

in America, with his

PARLOR CONCERT TROUPE,

will give entertainments, in conjunction
with his latest novelty,

MASTER
BONNIE RUNNELLS!

the great New York sensation, from Niblo's
Garden Theater, the

Funniest Dutchman!

on the stage, at

VACAVILLE,

Thursday and Friday evenings, October 8th
and 9th, 1874, and at

DIXON,

Saturday and Monday evenings, October 10th
and 12th. Also at

Woodland and Knight's Landing

shortly.

—o—

Popular Price of Admission, 50 cts.

—o—

A. F. BAILEY, Business Manager.
CHAS. B. TENNILL, Advance Agent.

The Weekly Solano Republican *published the advertisement October 8, 1874. According to their review, Vivian was "The very best comic vocalist we ever heard," and comparing Vivian to other performers, "ordinary entertainments of the kind sink into insignificance." Solano County Archives. Photograph of Charles Algernon Sidney Vivian, California State Library.*

grab Roe by the shoulders to prevent him from fighting. Myers said, "If you want to fight, now have a fair fight, and don't three or four of you jump on the poor devil and kill him in the street because he has no friends." Myers then allowed another man to seize Roe to drag him away from the fight. However Roe broke free, fell down and in getting up, caught sight of Myers standing a few feet away. Roe swore at Myers and drew his gun. Myers ran but Roe shot him in the head from behind. Everyone stood stunned for a few moments, then Armstrong said, "In the name of God, kill or take that man." Roe ran, chased by some men, but was caught by the marshal and jailed. According to the newspaper, Roe had a history of violence: ". . . whilst under the influence of liquor he became wild and passionate. Fearfully indeed has he accounted for this indulgence."[4]

The major problem with Luzena's account is the timing. She said this lynching happened on the second day after she journeyed down from Nevada City. However, the Nevada City fire was on March 11, and the lynching occurred two

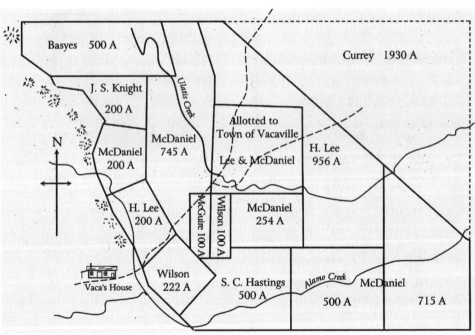

The earliest known parcel map of the Vaca Valley is dated 1852. The parcel labeled "Wilson.222 A" is the Wilsons' first 200-acre purchase plus a later acquisition. In addition to the two parcels shown here, they had also begun to buy town lots. The county road just north of the Wilsons' 222 acres lies roughly along the path of present-day Interstate 80. Vaca's adobe was located near the westbound Peaceful Glen exit of that freeway. Map by Bill Spurlock, drawn from Vacaville Heritage Council.

weeks earlier on February 24. Was she really present at both events? Or did she perhaps hear so often of the hanging that the story became hers? Was she in Sacramento for a business trip during February, then back in Nevada City two weeks later? She described both the fire and the lynching so well that she seems a credible eyewitness. Since no other lynchings are recorded in the Sacramento papers in early 1851 and so many details correspond, the Roe lynching must be the one she meant. In any case, both events occurred much as she reported and it would be a rare oral history that did not contain a few conundrums of this sort to perplex future generations.

The Wilsons turned west to find their next home. They chose not to swim their mules across the Sacramento River as stock trader Jerome Davis did; if they had, they might have decided to settle near Davisville, the town named for him. His 8,000-acre rancho, Laguna de Santos Calle, is today the site of the University of California at Davis. Instead, the Wilsons went upstream to Knight's Landing to cross the Sacramento, and so arrived in the fertile Vaca Valley.

Vaca Valley, Solano County

Luzena described a peaceful walk through today's Yolo County toward the foothills of the coastal range; the beauty of the countryside and the colors of spring were delightful. The tall oats through which they passed provided food for herds of "half-wild" Spanish cattle as well as the abundant wildlife. William Pleasants described the hills teeming with plant and animal life:

> Hundreds of elk could be seen in a single herd, and antelope were equally numerous, while great flocks of wild geese covered thousands of acres of ground at a time. Deer were plentiful and quite tame. Of these as many as a hundred or more could be seen in half a day's hunt. And I must not forget to mention that royal beast, the grizzly bear. This region was his home, and for years . . . he continued to challenge our right to oust him from it.

Luzena mentioned that Mason's rifle supplied the meat for her table from this bounty. The Pleasants men hunted game to sell for meat in Sacramento at 25 to 50 cents per pound, and a 400-pound bear was a profitable prize indeed.

What evidence of human habitation did the Wilsons see in the Vaca Valley? William Pleasants and his family settled north of Vaca Valley four months before the Wilsons arrived and again he provides clues:

Where Vacaville is now there was one small house, owned and occupied by a Mrs. McGuire. Two of the Longs also lived in that neighborhood. In Lagoon Valley, there were two Spanish families, named, respectively, Barker and Panier [Vaca and Peña] These were the only settlers within twenty miles of our house.

James McGuire and his wife had opened a primitive hotel in 1850, and William McDaniel had erected a building in the town plat which he laid out that year. The logical location for a hotel business was the town center, so the Wilsons probably established their open-air hotel near these two other buildings along the banks of the Ulatis Creek.

The Wilsons made their first real estate deal in Solano County April 21, 1851, exactly one month and ten days after the disastrous Nevada City fire. Obviously Luzena did not languish too long in that mountain cabin recovering her health, nor did the family linger in Sacramento contemplating their future. In a bond recorded that spring day, L. B. Mizner and William McDaniel agreed to sell two hundred acres to Mason Wilson. The parcel lay along Alamo Creek, near the present Three Oaks Community Center, about a mile west of the town plat. This property was just south of the county road that ran from Sacramento to Benicia, close to Manuel Vaca's adobe. Seven months later, Mason bought three squares of property in the town plat as well as one hundred acres south of town; this plot lay between the town and the first property he purchased. By Christmastime, the Wilsons had enacted their plan to "buy land and settle."

Mason's hay business had good potential for profit, but it would take time to cut, bale and take the oat hay to market. The family needed cash immediately so Luzena promptly set up her hotel. Wilson's Hotel seemed to thrive from the beginning, providing steady income and establishing Luzena's reputation as a hostess. She was pleased that her guests praised her cooking and enjoyed her company. Mr. Thaddeus Hoppin, a Yolo County farmer who came to California with his brothers, was one such admirer. After polishing off one of Luzena's breakfasts, he rated it well compared to the cucumber and sour milk cuisine at "Allford's." He was probably referring to Landy and Sarah Alford who lived in Rockville, in the Suisun Valley, near present-day Fairfield. The Alfords arrived in California in 1846, the same year the ill-fated Donner party was on the trail. According to family legend, the Alfords considered that party inexperienced and slow-paced and avoided them.[5] The land for the Rockville Chapel and Cemetery, which is now State Historical Landmark No. 779, was purchased from the Alfords: $50 for five acres. Sarah is buried there and her picture hangs on the wall of the stone chapel.

Sarah Duke Alford, dressed for her daughter Adeline's wedding in 1863. Nine children were born to Sarah and her husband, Landy. In her later years, Sarah lived with Adeline and enjoyed rocking on the porch while smoking her clay pipe. When visitors came, she would conceal her lit pipe in her apron, thus earning the nickname "Patches" because of the numerous burn holes she had to mend. Frank Pangburn.

Luzena said the Wolfskills lived twelve miles away and were her "nearest American neighbors," a statement that is perplexing and probably not true. The McGuire, Long and Pleasants families were all closer than twelve miles and early records also mention the pioneer names Dutton, Hollingsworth, Lyon, Hoppe and Patton in Vaca Valley. Both Hollingsworth and Long were married. Either Luzena chose not to notice the other American settlers and women at the time or failed to recall them in later years.

Undoubtedly she had a real affection for Permelia Wolfskill who came west with her husband Mathus in 1850 to live on the Wolfskill ranch near the present town of Winters. Mathus worked the land there with his brothers William, John, Sachel and Milton. In 1866 Permelia and Mathus moved their family to the Suisun Valley where they bought seven hundred acres and grew a wide variety of fruit and nut crops. Luzena regarded Permelia as a true friend for twenty-five years, and mourned her passing when Permelia died in 1876 at age sixty-six.

The entire Wolfskill clan was hard-working, honest and enterprising—the sort of people Luzena admired—but John Wolfskill made the most enduring impact on the community. He was the first American settler in Solano County and was a widely respected and valuable citizen. He gave shelter and aid to those in need, including some survivors of the Donner party and also a widow with eight children. But it is his contribution to agriculture that has formed his most lasting legacy. He was the pioneer grower of Solano County's fruit crops, planti-

John R. Wolfskill. Fairfield Public Library.

ng some as early as 1842. He was evangelical in his efforts, encouraging other settlers to cultivate orchards and sharing his propagating stock. John Wolfskill enjoyed "assisting nature in making a tree or plant," in the words of his son Edward.[6] The list of orchard crops he cultivated included apricots, grapes, figs, walnuts, and citrus trees such as orange, lime, lemon and citron. His name is preserved today at the Wolfskill Tract, a horticultural preserve and research facility owned by the University of California at Davis. Crops grow there in the same soil that the Wolfskill brothers worked 150 years ago, not far from where their tule house stood. Olive trees planted by John still grow on the property, a fitting tribute.

NOTES

1. Frank Marryat, *Mountains and Molehills*, 117.

2. John F. Morse, *First History of Sacramento*, 100.

3. *Sacramento Transcript*, February 26, 1851, 2.

4. *Sacramento Transcript*, February 28, 1851, 2.

5. Unpublished letter from Frank Pangburn, great-great grandson of Stephen Landers (Landy) Alford and Sarah Duke Alford, May 13, 2002.

6. Joann Leach Larkey, *Winters: A Heritage of Horticulture, A Harmony of Purpose*, 14.

Luzena: VACA VALLEY
1851–1855

O UR NEAREST NEIGHBORS WERE THE MEMBERS OF THE SPANISH COLONY, who lived only three-quarters of a mile away, in the little Laguna Valley. The lord of the soil, the original owner of all the land included in the grant on which we lived, was Manuel Vaca, and around him clustered the Spanish population of great or lesser note. Some of their adobe houses still remain, in unpleasing, barren, squalid desolation, a rude and fast-decaying monument to the vanished grandeur of Spanish California, and a shelter to American settlers of even less energy and enterprise than the "greasers." About us in all directions roamed herds of cattle and droves of mustangs, which constituted the wealth of the settlement and a whole day's hard riding about the grant would not reveal half the extent of their four-footed possessions. Even at that early day some portions of the original grant had already passed from Vaca to American owners. Today of all that great body of fertile valley and leagues of pasture land scarcely more that two or three hundred acres can be found in the possession of his heirs.

The Mexican character of slothfulness and procrastination assisted materially to undermine their financial stability, and they succumbed to the strategy and acuteness of the American trader. It was but a few years till the proud rulers of the valley were the humblest subjects of the new monarchs, reduced from affluence almost to beggary by too greatly trusted Yankees.

At the time we arrived in the valley, however, the "greaser" element, as it has since been called, was in its pristine glory. All the accompaniments of Spanish happiness were to be found in the small precinct occupied by their dwellings. An army of vaqueros congregated every day about the settlement, smoked cigarettes, ran races, played cards for high stakes, and drank bad whisky in unlimited quantities. The man of position felt proud of his patrician blood, and condescended when he addressed his surrounding inferiors. He wore a broad sombrero, gold-laced jacket and wide bell-decked pantaloons, girt his waist with a flaming sash, wore jangling at his heels, large, clanking, silver spurs, swung a lariat with unerring aim, and in the saddle looked a centaur. The belles of the valley coquetted with the brave riders, threw at them melting glances from their eyes, and whispered sweet nothings in the melodious Spanish tongue. I was always treated with extreme consideration by the Spanish people, and they quite frequently invited me to participate in their dances and feast, which they gave to celebrate their great occasions. We had been in the valley only about two months, when Senor Vaca came riding over one morning to ask me, by the aid of an interpreter, to attend a ball to be given that night at his house. I was quite unfamiliar with the manner and customs of the Spanish people, and my acceptance of the cordial and pressing invitation was prompted quite as much by curiosity as by my friendly feelings for my neighbors.

When we arrived at the adobe house the light streamed through open windows and doors far out into the night and revealed, tethered all about, the saddle-horses of the guests and lit up many black-eyed, smiling faces, looking to see how the Americans would be received. Don Manuel with his daughter, greeted us with all the ceremony and courtesy of a Spanish grandee and showed us to the place of honor. We were ushered into a long room illuminated with tallow dips, destitute of furniture, with the exception of the two or three chairs reserved exclusively for the use of the American visitors. On either side were many mats, on which reclined with careless grace and ease the flirting belle and beau and the wrinkled duennas of the fiesta. The musical accompaniment to the dancing, which had already begun, was played upon guitar and tambourine, and the laughing, chattering, happy crowd swayed and turned in wave-like undulation to the rhythm of a seductive waltz. They fluttered their silken vari-colored scarfs, and bent their lithe bodies in graceful dances which charmed my cotillion and quadrille-accustomed eyes. The young ladies were dressed in true Mexican costume; snowy chemises of soft fine linen, cut low, displayed the plump necks, leaving bare the dimpled arms; bright hued silk petticoats in great plaid patterns and shawls and scarfs of brilliant scarlet, set off in contrast their glossy, jet hair, their red lips, and their sparkling, tigerish, changing eyes. The men in holiday attire of velvet jackets of royal purple and emerald green, profusely trimmed with gold and silver braids, were as gaudy in color and picturesque in appearance as the feminine portion of the assembly. The refreshments comprised strangely compounded but savory Spanish stews, hot with chilies, great piles of tortillas, and gallons of only tolerable whisky. Near midnight they were served informally. Some of the guests ate reclining on their mats, some standing about the long, low table, some lounging in door-ways and window-seats—all laughing, talking, coquetting and thoroughly enjoying the passing minutes, forgetful of yesterday, heedless of tomorrow, living only in the happy present. Among the prominent and honored guests were members of the most wealthy and influential Spanish families of the country. I remember well the pretty faces and manly figures of the Armijos, Picos, Peñas, and Berryessas, who have long since been gathered in peace to their fathers, or are still living, holding prominent places in various California communities.

The vaqueros who rode up and down about the country stopped often at our place, and were very kind and friendly. Many a quarter of freshly killed beef or mutton, game caught in the valley, or birds snared in the mountains, found their way from their hands to my not over-well stocked larder. Once they brought me a young elk, that I might have it about the place for a pet. I was delighted with the gift, and took it out toward the corral, intending to keep it with the cows. Imagine my surprise and consternation when, as I approached the gate, meek, patient old mulley, who had followed us across the plains and lived through fire and flood, lashed her tail from side to side, broke into a gallop, scaled an eight foot fence at a single bound and only stopped her frightened run when she was three miles from home. After that I gave up my intention of adding an elk to my domestic collection of animals, and declined all further gifts of the kind. The vaquero and his horse were inseparable; even while he drank his whisky at the roadside "deadfull" he retained his hold on the lariat of the horse grazing fifty feet away outside. He ate, drank, and slept in the saddle; and even if he lay down under a tree for the night, the horse was in constant requisition for a breathless gallop across country after the stampeding cattle.

Toward the end of the summer months, as we began to look for the early rains, the matter of house-building absorbed all our attention. Lumber was very scarce and very high in price, and all that we got was hauled from Benicia, a distance of thirty miles, and greater part of our savings was used up in the construction of the rudest kind of a shelter. I had grown so accustomed to sleeping in the open air, that the first night we slept under a roof I absolutely suffered from a sense of suffocation, although there were neither doors nor windows to the structure. All during the summer my hotel had prospered and made money, while my husband kept hard at work making hay. At the end of the season, he had cut and baled and hauled the long fifteen miles to Cache Slough, two hundred tons of hay and it lay there awaiting shipment to San Francisco. But alas for all our hopes, the rains came unexpectedly, and the water rising in tules, carried away again all the labor of the year and the money on which we had depended to pay partly for the land we had bought. The hay was a total loss, and we had only the refuge of harder work at the hotel business and farming for next year.

Trouble seemed to follow us relentlessly; we had scarcely moved into our little frame house under the oak, when the Land Commissioners met in San Francisco to settle or accept the surveys of the Spanish grants. Among the disputed boundary lines were those of the grant upon which we had bought. The commissioners had decided at first that the land upon which we lived was included in the grant, but the news had scarcely reached us when other testimony bearing on the case was heard, and the decision was reversed. The news came to Benicia at night, and long before daylight there came knocks at the door calling me up, and I was busy until long after the usual breakfast time satisfying the hunger of the unusually large crowd of travelers. My husband was away in Sacramento, and therefore I did not learn till later in the day the cause of this sudden immigration. By night a whole party of surveyors had staked off half the valley and all the land we had bought, and a band of squatters had built a rough cabin half a mile from us. When my husband returned at night he was furious, and he swore that he would either have the land or kill every man who disputed his ownership. Before it was light he left the house on his errand of ejectment, taking with him a witness, in case he should be killed or be forced to kill the squatters. He kissed me good-bye, hardly expecting to come back to me alive, for the squatters, many of whom knew and feared his reckless and determined purpose, would not have hesitated to dispose of him with a bullet.

He walked straight to their cabin, and pushing aside the blanket hung for a door, found the intruders, six in number, sound asleep, and their guns standing loaded, ready for use, near at hand. Slipping softly in, he secured the six guns, and then, covering the sleepers with his own weapon, waked them. They were of course enraged but helpless, and at his command filed silently out of the cabin. Then, still under the pitiless aim of that steady gun, they silently and unresistingly watched the demolition and removal of their mushroom house. When the last stick of wood and scrap of material had been dragged away, the gun was lowered, and they were given a solemn warning never again to attempt the unlawful seizure of another man's property under pain of death. The foiled squatters stormed and raved and vowed vengeance, but we were troubled no more by that party. Others, with as little regard for the rights of property-owners, were ready to attempt, and did attempt, the same wholesale theft of land, but were disposed of in as summary a manner. The trouble thus begun grew into a perfect war, in courts and out of courts. Men who paid for their lands were determined to hold them at any cost, and everybody went armed to the teeth, ready to defend his claim. The decisions of the Land Commissioners kept us in a state of continuous ferment, and for years we had not only a hard struggle to keep our land, but were in constant terror of the murderous shots of the infuriated men who desired to eject us. The "squatters" were so much the topic of common conversation among us that even the children, left to invent their own amusements, used to play at being "squatters." Once, had I not rescued my youngest son, he would have been hanged, in mimicry of the punishment not unusually discussed as a salient remedy for the "squatter troubles."

The capital of the State was removed to Benicia about the time that we moved to Vaca Valley, and that point being not far distant, we were on the route of constant travel, and among the men who stopped with us often were some who, even then, owned large tracts of land in the country, and many of whom have since become well known to the public, either through political position or great wealth. Among them were Judge S. C. Hastings, who still lives in San Francisco, and who has since amassed a great fortune, a monument of energy and business shrewdness. Judge Murray Morrison dispensed justice in our district courts; Judge Curry was the owner of a great deal of valuable property; Judge Wallace meted out punishment to offenders. Mr. L. B. Mizner, who still lives in Benicia, was an early traveler; Mr. Paul Shirley and he were for years the most dashing beaux of the scattered young ladies of the upper country.

The map of the town of Vacaville had been filed some years before we settled there, but it was still some time before enough people came there to justify us in asking for a postoffice or giving the place its name.

The second Christmas of our stay I gave a dinner party, and invited all the Americans in the valley; even then I entertained only five guests. My dinner party was considered very fine for the time. My cook was a negro of the blackest hue, who had formerly cooked for some army officer, and was accustomed to skirmishing, as he expressed it. The menu included onion soup, roast elk, a fricasse of lamb, boiled onion, the home-grown luxury of radishes, lettuce and parsley, dried-apple pies, and rice pudding. Fowls were too rare and valuable to be sacrificed, as yet, to the table, and probably had they been killed would have defied mastication, for they were, like ourselves, pioneers.

Piute Indian

Top: *At spring and fall roundups the vaqueros showcased their superb horsemanship and skill with the riata. These lassos were made of three strips of specially prepared bullock hide. Strips were carefully cut in a circular pattern from the center of the hide outwards, to avoid any splicing, then braided together into a very strong 50 or 60-foot length. California State Library.*

Left: *Under Spanish colonial law, Indians such as this Paiute vaquero were not permitted to ride horses. However, the padres at the early Missions needed skilled labor and hence trained many Indians as horsemen; after the Missions were secularized, these men found work on the ranchos. Rose Coombs, a Peña descendant, stated that her family had Indian vaqueros. The Vacas and Peñas also used Indian labor for house construction and domestic service. Carl Mautz Collection.*

19 *Trouble seemed to follow us relentlessly . . .*

LIKE LUZENA, JUAN MANUEL VACA WAS DRAWN TO CALIFORNIA by a dream. According to family lore, as a young man in Spain he envisioned "a valley of his own where he could establish himself as supreme lord and master of as much land as his eyes could survey."[1] He arrived in the valley that would eventually bear his name about ten years before the Wilsons. Vaca and his partner, Juan Felipe Peña, were granted ten Spanish leagues by the Mexican governor. The two gentlemen immediately settled with their large families on the more than 44,000 acres of land in present-day Solano County.

Life on their new property was ideal. Their adobe homes were open to travelers and invited guests, and hospitality varied between warm and lavish, as Luzena observed. Weddings and other celebrations were occasions for fiestas which might last for a week. The annual cattle roundup was always accompanied by such a feast. Horses were vital to the vaqueros whose herds were their wealth. The hides and tallow were harvested for trade, but the meat had little commercial value in the early days. The cattle required little supervision, leaving the families free to enjoy themselves and the blessings of the good life. The adobe homes of the two Dons were the center of family life; as children married, they established homes elsewhere on the family lands.[2]

This paradise did not last long. The Mexican–American War brought a change of government and upset the idyllic world of the Californios. Although the treaty ending the war promised respect for the Mexican land grants, the grant owners had to engage in protracted legal battles to prove their claims under U.S. law. Vaca's legal position would have been improved if he had surveyed his land with precise instruments; the vague boundary descriptions and imprecise language in the original grant led to protracted wrangling.

Since both Vaca and Peña were illiterate they signed all documents with an "X." They were at a disadvantage in legal battles. Neither was fluent in English, so they had to rely upon interpreters and their lawyers, some of whom appeared more interested in their own profits than in preserving their clients' lands. The usual attorney fee in these cases was a percentage of the land disputed, and the fee was collected regardless of the outcome. Luzena noted that her Spanish neighbors were cheated by "too greatly trusted Yankees," and some of these were certainly attorneys. Others were squatters hungry for land and unscrupulous enough to partake of the generous hospitality of their hosts before taking advantage of them. Señor Vaca was a gentleman of the old school, more than sixty years of age, with the manners of a "Spanish grandee" according to Luzena. Nothing in his background prepared him to deal with the new reality that swept into California after the discovery of gold. The easy-going ways of the Californios soon began to look like "slothfulness and procrastination," as Luzena put it.

The Spanish era with its fiestas and fandangos was drawing to a close as land battles played out in the courts. Engraving from the 1850s, private collection.

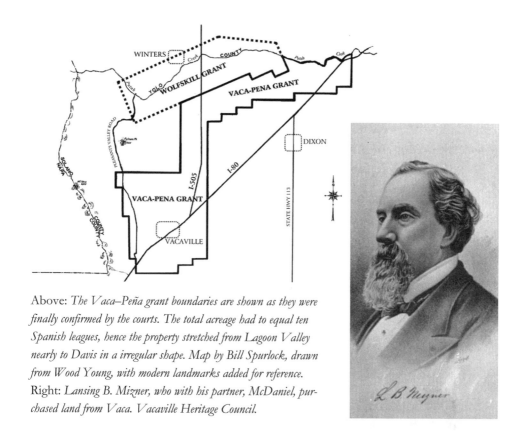

Above: *The Vaca–Peña grant boundaries are shown as they were finally confirmed by the courts. The total acreage had to equal ten Spanish leagues, hence the property stretched from Lagoon Valley nearly to Davis in a irregular shape. Map by Bill Spurlock, drawn from Wood Young, with modern landmarks added for reference.*
Right: *Lansing B. Mizner, who with his partner, McDaniel, purchased land from Vaca. Vacaville Heritage Council.*

There was also outright prejudice against the Mexican and Spanish residents in early California. Luzena acknowledged her fascination with her exotic Spanish neighbors, praised their courtesy, valued their friendship, and enjoyed their hospitality. But she still used the term "greasers" to refer the general Mexican and Spanish-speaking population, an epithet that was regrettably common as early as 1846. Even the state legislature used this slur in an anti-vagrancy law in 1855, defining vagrants as "all persons who [were] commonly known as 'Greasers' or the issue of Spanish or Indian blood." Other legislation subjected California-born Mexicans to the Foreign Miner's Tax, even though they were U.S. citizens by law. In effect, they became "foreigners in their own land."[3]

Eight months before the Wilsons arrived in the valley, Vaca made a significant sale to William McDaniel. The deed granted McDaniel nine square miles of land with the condition that a town be laid out and named for Vaca, but he made at least two mistakes. He acted alone, which angered his partner Peña, and the rift between them undoubtedly made them even more vulnerable to manipulation. Even worse, Vaca claimed that he did not understand the document he signed. He published the following in the *California Gazette* in May 1851:

> *Caution. I hereby notify all persons, not to purchase any lands from William McDaniel, which he claims to have purchased from me under a title which he obtained from me under false pretenses and I shall institute suit against him to annul the title so fraudulently obtained by him.*[4]

Vaca evidently thought he was selling one square mile of land instead of nine. McDaniel responded with a suit for libel, and another fight began. By this time,

Above: *Portrait of Juan Manuel Vaca.* Right: *Juan Felipe Peña. Vacaville Heritage Council.*

Suisun Valley, November_____185 2.

Mr._____

Suisun,

Sir :

The Lands which you have taken possession of and have settled upon, belong to me ; and I hereby **WARN** *you, against all losses you already have, or hereafter may, render yourself liable to ; by continuing to occupy, cultivate or improve the said Lands, without my written sanction.*

Your obt servt.

A. A. RITCHIE.

Above: *Letter written by Archibald Alexander Ritchie of nearby Suisun Valley, another early Solano County landowner. He tried to warn squatters off his property with stern language; Mason Wilson preferred the persuasive power of a shotgun. The Bancroft Library.*
Left: *John Currey, Peña's attorney. California State Library.*

McDaniel and his partner Lansing B. Mizner had already begun to sell the land in question. Mason Wilson made his first purchase from the two men in April, a month before Vaca protested publicly.

The peaceful valley that the Wilsons viewed that first spring morning harbored conflicts that would envelop them for years. Around the time they arrived, a State Land Commission was formed in Benicia to sort out the land grant disputes and uncertainty prevailed. Vaca and Peña filed their claim February 20, 1852, and it was rejected November 15, 1853. It was then the ragtag army of squatters arrived on the Wilsons' land, prompting Mason to evict them at gunpoint. This legal setback still did not shake the Wilsons' resolve to hold the land, although Mason had to take up arms repeatedly to defend it.

An appeal was immediately filed and new legal counsel took over. John Currey became the primary attorney for Peña. Since there were additional interested parties, including Vaca and other purchasers of the disputed lands, numerous co-counsels shared in the legal fees but not the work, according to Currey. Mexican land grant cases were Currey's specialty, and he proved to be a thorough investigator and able advocate. He prevailed in the appeal to the Land Commission by sorting out the land surveys and clearing up the contradictory language. Subsequent appeals to the U.S. District Court upheld this favorable decision and the U.S. Supreme Court added its stamp of approval by the end of 1855. The final assurance came in June 1858 when President James Buchanan signed a patent for the Los Putos Grant, comprising 44,383 acres, belonging to Juan Manuel Vaca and Juan Felipe Peña. The gamble that Mason and Luzena took had paid off after seven years of anxiety. For Vaca, the ending was not so happy; he died just a few months before his title was confirmed.

The Wilsons did not foresee any of this in 1851, since they were focused upon the need to earn money and build a home before winter arrived. Luzena said most of the profits from that first summer's business were used to buy lumber in Benicia for a house. Their carpenter was Romulus Kennedy, who claimed that this was the first wooden house built in Vacaville. Kennedy, a native of New York State, came to California in 1850. He soon became disillusioned with mining and took up his trade as a builder in the Sacramento area. He came to Vacaville for the Wilson project and returned to Sacramento upon its completion. Eventually an injury forced him to retire from carpentering, and he returned to Vacaville in 1858 to manage the Wilson House, which was by then a two-story brick structure. He moved to Lakeport in 1864 and lived out his days there.[5]

The wooden house did double duty as the family residence and a hotel. One guest was Judge Currey, the same man whose legal efforts were vital in securing the Wilsons' clear title to their land. Currey had a law practice in Benicia, but later moved his family onto the land he had obtained from Vaca and Peña. This property was located near Dixon and is still held by the Currey family. Currey ran for public office several times, including an unsuccessful pursuit of the governorship in 1859. In 1863 he was elected to the California Supreme Court, and three years later became chief justice, serving two years before resuming a private legal practice. Currey was a serious man who continued to take an interest in the courts and wrote on legal questions long after his retirement. He died in Dixon in 1912 at age ninety-eight.

Serranus Clinton Hastings. California State Library.

Another hotel visitor that Luzena listed was Serranus Clinton Hastings (1814–1893), the first chief justice of the California Supreme Court. Originally from New York, he had settled in Iowa, serving as a U.S. congressman and chief justice of that state before emigrating to Benicia in 1849. He rose rapidly to power and became Chief Justice in January 1850. After two years in office, he became Attorney General, all the while energetically pursuing a private legal and business practice. His land grant cases netted him a considerable real estate empire, and he gradually reduced his law practice to focus on managing his properties in numerous Northern California counties. His lasting legacy is Hastings College of the Law, established as the first law school of the University of California in 1878. He had a large family with his first wife, Azalea, and they enjoyed travel, horses, and the good life in general. After Azalea died, Judge Hastings remained a widower for eight years and then astonished his friends by marrying Lillian Kunst, who was some fifty years younger than he. Always known as a witty man, the judge evidently bore well the amusement this alliance afforded his family. When he informed his son Robert that Lillian was expecting a child,

Robert responded, "And Father, whom do you suspect?"[6] Additional drama arose from a lawsuit brought by another woman who had nursed the judge through an illness and had expectations of marrying him herself. His death set in motion a series of court actions over the division of his estate and wealth.

Luzena seemed proud to have known so many prominent men. She mentioned Judge Murray Morrison who began his legal career in Sacramento. He represented the landowners Rogers and Burnett, whose eviction of the squatter Madden in Sacramento kindled the 1850 squatter riot. While there, Morrison married Jennie White, daughter of the first Assembly Speaker of the state. They moved to San Francisco and eventually settled in Southern California where he served as a state legislator and judge of the District Court. He died in 1871 and his heartbroken wife followed him in death only five days later. Other visitors included Judge Wallace of the Seventh District Court, and Paul Shirley who made a name in both business and politics. Starting out in Benicia as a partner with Judge Hastings in a lumber business, Shirley in 1869 bought the ferry that connected Benicia to Port Costa. As the years passed he acquired sizeable real estate holdings. He served as Solano County's first sheriff as a Whig, then a Democrat, and later was state senator for Marin and Contra Costa Counties. Eventually he was appointed warden at San Quentin. Luzena was also acquainted with Lansing B. Mizner of Benicia, an attorney whose name appears as a census taker, land speculator, lawyer and state senator. With his partner McDaniel, Mizner sold the Wilsons their first parcel of land in the Vaca Valley.

Although Luzena worked in her hotel, she also hired help. In 1852, she hosted a Christmas banquet for five Americans in the area, a dinner that is annually remembered in modern Vacaville by serving onion soup during the community Christmas tree-lighting ceremony. Her cook at that time was a black man whose name is not given. Perhaps he was Samuel Sipples who was certainly in the Wilsons' employ a few months later. Sipples eventually became disgruntled and filed suit against Mason for unpaid wages. Mr. Sipples' court complaint states that he worked at the Wilson's Hotel from April 1853 to January 1854 and should have been paid $540 for those nine months, since his salary was $60 per month. Through his attorney, Sipples also claimed wages of $75 per month for the following nine months; he asked for a total of $1,215, plus interest and court fees. Mason Wilson responded that Mr. Sipples was drunk much of the time, didn't work regularly and didn't even earn his board and keep; in fact, for six weeks straight he was sick as well as drunk. According to Wilson, the agreement was that Sipples would work for one year for $600 and not drink. To bolster the case, the Wilson ledger book was displayed, showing that Sipples owed $411.25, itemized purchases for drinks, tobacco, clothes and food. Mason claimed he had offered the cook $50 and full forgiveness of the debt to settle the matter, but Samuel refused and filed suit. Beyond the filings of the briefs, no further legal action was recorded, so presumably they reached some accord.[7] Samuel Sipples was in Vallejo in 1860, where, at age sixty, he was working as a servant in the home of Captain John B. Frisbie, the city's founding father. As for the Wilsons, in later years they continued to employ domestic help in the hotel, including servants from Ireland, China, and various American states.

NOTES

1. Helen Dormody Crystal, "The Beginnings of Vacaville," 49.
2. Wood Young, *Vaca–Peña Los Putos Rancho and the Peña Adobe*, 6–9.
3. Ronald T. Takaki, *A Different Mirror: A History of Multicultural America*, 178.
4. Richard Rico, "Is Vacaville Built on a Foundation of Fraud?," *Vacaville Reporter*, August 16, 1981, 6–7.
5. *History of Napa and Lake Counties, California*, 256–257.
6. Johnson, J. Edward, *History of the Supreme Court Justices of California*, 28.
7. Court File No. 323, Solano County Archives.

20

Luzena: VACA VALLEY
1855–1878

A S TIME WENT ON, WE AND OUR FEW NEIGHBORS began to wish for educational advantages for our children, and by paying double tuition for each child we managed to secure a teacher—sound in mind, but defective in body, he having lost a leg and an eye—to start a school in a little blue cotton house under a tree. The trustees of this school of six pupils were Mr. Ed. McGary (he afterward moved to Green Valley and after amassing a substantial fortune, again to San Francisco where he still lives), Mr. Eugene Price (he died some years ago, a wealthy resident of Chicago) and my husband. The canvas building was shortly replaced by a wooden structure and this in turn by a larger one; and the school thus started developed some years later into the Pacific Methodist College, which was for many years one of the foremost educational institutions of California.

For a good many years after we came to Vaca Valley there were not enough families in the immediate vicinity to induce a doctor to settle there. Although the climate might safely be called the healthiest in the State, people once in a great while would get sick. A physician who made a desperate effort to make a living there and failed, left his medicine-chest in liquidation of his long-standing board bill, and thereafter I came to act as general practitioner and apothecary for the neighborhood, and my judgment on diseases was accepted with as much faith and my prescriptions followed with more readiness that is now often accorded to the most learned members of the medical fraternity. I dealt out blue-mass, calomel, and quinine to patients from far and near; inspected tongues and felt pulses, until I grew so familiar with the business that I almost fancied myself a genuine doctor. I don't think I ever killed anybody, and I am quite sure I cured a good many of patients. Indeed, they grew so accustomed to my ministrations that, even after a good physician settled among us, the sick people used not infrequently to ask me if they should take the medicine that he prescribed; and I believe that if the matter had come to an actual choice, they would have followed my advice in preference to his.

The Spanish population gradually vanished before the coming immigration. The thick-walled adobe houses, which sheltered under one roof horses and men, crumbled away and mingled with the dust. The vaquero and his bands of Spanish cattle fled to wider ranges. The plow turned the sod where the brilliant wild flowers had bloomed for ages undisturbed, and silken corn and golden wheat ripened in the little valley. Year by year more acres of the fertile land were laid under cultivation. The canvas tent was followed by a tiny, unpainted redwood cabin with a dirt floor, and that in turn by more pretentious homes. It was years before the title of the land was established, and we were kept in continual commotion through the persistent efforts of squatters to obtain possession. The surveys of the Spanish owners were very imperfect and caused a world of trouble and annoyance to their successors. The usual mode of measurement in early days, before surveyors and surveying instruments were in the country, was for a vaquero to take a fresh mustang and gallop an hour in any direction. The distance thus traversed was called ten miles. Smaller distances were subdivisions of the hour's ride; and, as the speed of the horse was variable you may easily see that the survey thus made would be a very irregular one and would be likely, as it did, to give rise to many complications in later transfers of the land.

The valley was settled principally by emigrants from Missouri and Arkansas, and they brought with them the shiftless ways of farming and housekeeping prevalent in the West and South, which have, in a measure, prevented the improvement and advancement that might have been expected from so fertile and productive a country. I remember as an illustration of the principles of early housekeeping, being called to help take care of a neighbor who was very ill. I sat up all night by the sick woman in company with another neighbor, a volunteer nurse. Growing hungry toward morning we concluded to get breakfast, so I sent the daughter of the house, a girl of seventeen years, to bring me some cream to make biscuits. She was gone a long time, and I waited with my hands in the flour for her to come back. Finally she made her appearance with the cream, and when

I asked the cause of the delay, she answered, "Well, old Bob was in the cream, and I had to stop and scrape him off."

To emphasize the statement, "old Bob," the cat, came in wet from his involuntary cream bath. I made the bread with water that I pumped myself. The out-door management of the men was as badly conducted as the indoor system of their wives. A general air of dilapidation seemed to pervade and cling to the houses and barns of the farmer from the West. He sat cross-legged on the fence and smoked a clay pipe in company with the "old woman," while the pigs and chickens rooted and scratched unmolested in his front garden. The Western farmers still, in some few instances, hold possession, and from the highway as you pass you may detect the unmistakable signs of their early training, but by far the greater part of the pioneer population has been succeeded by economical, industrious, energetic, thrifty families from the North and Canada, and they have converted the little valley into a cultivated and blooming garden. The redwood shanty has given way to large and well-built pleasant homes, furnished with comforts and often luxuries. Instead of the bare-footed, rag-covered urchins of early times, who ran wild with the pigs and calves, all along the roads one may see troops of rosy, well-clad children on their way to school. The old-time Sabbath amusements of riding bucking mustangs into the saloons, drinking all day at the various bars, running foot-races, playing poker, and finishing the day with a free fight are things of the past. The sobering influence of civilization has removed all such exciting but dangerous pastimes as playing scientific games of billiards by firing at the balls with a pistol, taking off the heads of the decanters behind the counter with a quick shot, and making the bar-keeper shiver for his well-curled hair. Now when the individual members of the enlightened population play cards, as perhaps they sometimes do, it is in the seclusion of the back-room, out of range of prying eyes.

We residents of Vaca Valley were an amusement-loving people in the early days of the settlement, and every few weeks saw a ball or party given, to which came all the younger portion of the surrounding families, and not seldom the town overflowed for the night with the buxom lads and lassies for thirty miles away. The largest room in the town— usually my dining room—was cleared to make room for the dancers, and they danced hard and long until daylight, and often the bright sunlight saw the participants rolling away in spring wagons, or galloping off on horseback to their distant homes. The costumes were, like the gathering, quite unique; the ladies came in calico dresses and calf boots; a ribbon was unusual, and their principal ornaments were good health and good nature; the gentlemen came ungloved, and sometimes coatless. But the fun was genuine, and when the last dance was turned off by the sleepy fiddler who kept time with his foot and called off in thundering tones the figures of the cotillions it was with a sigh of genuine regret that the many dancers said "good morning." Now the little town has grown civilized; when they give a party now, the young ladies come be-frizzled and montagued, with silk dresses, eight-button gloves, and French slippers with Pompadour heels; and the young men come in all the uninteresting solemnity of dress-coats.

The stages which ran every day from Sacramento to Napa and Benicia brought with them a stream of travelers and many new settlers to the valley. The arrival of the rattling, thundering old six-horse coach, with its load of grumbling, dusty passengers, and their accompanying poodle-dogs, canary birds, pet cats, parrots, Saratoga trunks and band-boxes, and the swaggering, self-important driver who handled the reins with consummate skill, and could only be bribed into amiability by frequent drinks, was the event of the day. All the dogs of the village welcomed its advent and saluted its departure with a chorus of howls; the ragged urchins along the dusty roads waved their battered hats and shouted at the stolid passengers; the old farmer rode up on his slow cob to wait its coming; the inquisitive girls peeped around the corner to see if perchance a new masculine attraction might be left in the town. With the stages went the rollicking, unassuming fun of the country, and with the railroads came in the aping of city airs and the following of city fashions.

For twenty-seven years I have called the little valley home, have watched with unfailing interest its growth and development. But few years elapsed until Vacaville was the center of a thriving country; the farm produce found its nearest market at the village stores; orchards and vineyards were planted, found profitable, were enlarged, flourished, and are today a source of wealth and constantly increasing revenue to the fortunate owners. But the "flush times" are all over; the trials and cares of the pioneer days are things of the past; the rags and tatters of my first days in California are well nigh forgotten in the ease and plenty of the present. The years have been full of hardships, but they have brought me many friends, and my memory of them is rich with pictures of their kind faces and echoes of their pleasant words. The dear old friends are falling asleep one by one; many of them are already lying quietly at rest under the friendly flower strewn California sod; day by day the circle narrows, and in a few more years there will be none of us left to talk over the "early days."

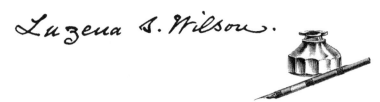

Luzena S. Wilson.

VIEW OF VACA VALLEY.

Above: *The 1937 edition of Luzena's memoir concluded with the engraving,* View of Vaca Valley *by McKowen and Bishop, which was based on an ambrotype. Vacaville Heritage Council.*

Facing page: *Luzena's signature is from the original manuscript. Special Collections, Mills College.*

Edgar F. Gillespie's store, Vacaville's first, had its start in a shed on the Wilson property. By 1858 when this daguerreotype was made, Gillespie had built a proper building and was the local Wells Fargo agent. In later years, Mason Wilson took on that job. California State Library.

21

The sobering influence of civilization . . .

THE WILSON FAMILY CIRCLE GREW DURING THE 1850s, as two more children were born to Luzena and Mason. In January 1855, a third son, Mason Jr., joined the family. And the *Solano County Herald* of May 2, 1857 tersely announced the advent of Correnah Morehead Wilson in the births column as follows: "On Friday, the 24th [of April], in Vacaville, the wife of Mr. Mason Wilson, of a daughter, weighing fifteen pounds." The weight of the baby can certainly not be confirmed, but suffice it to say that Correnah was Luzena's last child.

Education for the children was a priority; Thomas and Jay were in immediate need of instruction, as were other children of the town. No record has emerged of the school for six pupils which Luzena described. Besides Mason, two other men served as trustees of this tent school; one of them—Edward McGary—later became Thomas Wilson's father-in-law when Thomas married his schoolmate, Maggie McGary. Edward McGary owned substantial real estate and farmed as well. He was later a prominent citizen of Green Valley, where a road is named for him.

The trustees set up the school on a fee basis, since there was no public money for education at that time. Another group of parents set up a similar school east of town in the fall of 1853. Its story was told by a student, Edson Clarke, in his later years. He painted a lively portrait of frontier learning, Vacaville style. This school was located under an oak tree in an open field. (According to the Allison family papers, the school was about one and a half mile east of town on Hawkins' property.) The teacher was "a handsome young lady" staying with her sister who was married to a local rancher.

The teacher sat in a real chair, but for a desk she had an inverted barrel clothed in cal-
ico. Divers [diverse] milkstools, soap boxes and inverted buckets comprised the bulk of the

school furniture which, being movable, enabled the children to 'follow the shade.' There were less than a dozen pupils with less than a dozen textbooks—no two of a kind.

The students were fond of their pretty teacher, but she was gone in a month. A young suitor claimed her hand in marriage and school was dismissed. The next teacher was a man with an unfortunate flaw: "an uncontrollable appetite which led him to the nearest saloon at the close of every week." He lasted three weeks.[1]

Finally in 1855, James Wright Anderson, age twenty-four, was hired and a proper redwood one-room schoolhouse built under the oaks. Professor Anderson was surely not the disabled teacher that Luzena remembered; Edson Clarke took great delight in telling the story of a fistfight between Anderson and an angry parent. Anderson had punished a young scholar with a whipping and the aggrieved boy immediately fetched his father to press home his complaint; in short, the two men took the argument outside. The students, of course, ran to the windows. Although the professor was a foot shorter and some ninety pounds lighter than his challenger, he was an experienced boxer and defended himself well. After dodging many blows and tiring his opponent, Anderson finally was caught by a fist and began to bleed, at which point the father declared himself satisfied and sat down to regain his breath. Anderson returned to the class, having acquitted himself well in the eyes of all. Since the angry parent had not beaten their teacher, only landed a blow, and since Anderson had asserted and defended his authority in the classroom, the students decided that the Professor had actually won!

Before the school year ended, Anderson was invited to set up a school in the town of Vacaville, "a select school where only the higher branches would be taught. . . . Professor Anderson was duly installed as the principal of 'Ulatus Academy' . . . and was earning a salary of $300 a month," according to Edson Clarke. The Ulatis Academy absorbed the students from Anderson's original school, as well as the one the Wilsons had organized. Thomas Stanley Wilson was a graduate of Ulatis Academy, which was located near the corner of present day McClellan and East Main streets, on the south side of Ulatis Creek.

While teaching in this first district school, Anderson also served as the Solano County Superintendent of Schools. He later filled that same post in San Francisco, and also served as president of Hesperian College in Woodland. He capped his career by being elected on the Republican ticket as State Superintendent of Schools, holding the office from 1891 to 1894.

To provide for the family and supplement the hotel income, Mason pursued farming. He began by cutting and hauling oat hay in 1851, and as he acquired

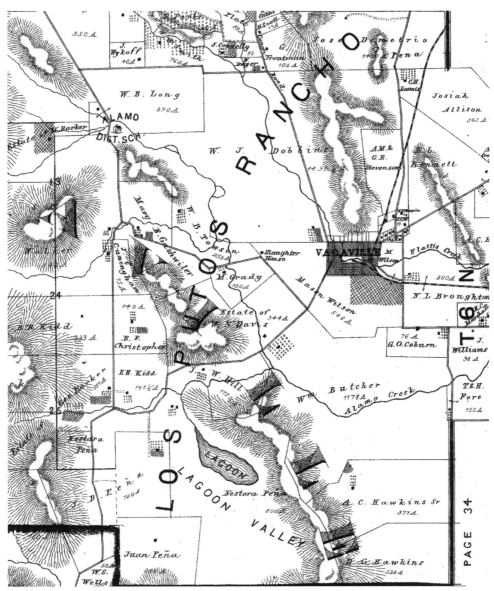

The Wilson property, shown in this 1877 map, surrounded the town plat on the east, south and west. W. J. Dobbins, Luzena's brother-in-law, owned the land north of town. In the upper right corner Josiah Allison's property is indicated, where his descendants established the Nut Tree Restaurant complex in the 1920s. Vacaville Museum.

An 1866 view of Vacaville shows the Wilson Hotel, the large, two story brick building at the far left of the photo. The vantage point is looking south from today's Monte Vista Avenue; the southern end of the Blue Ridge Mountains is just visible through the chimney smoke. Vacaville Museum.

acreage, he planted other grains such as wheat, barley and corn. Very little land was fenced in those days; the grain was protected from roaming cattle by digging a deep ditch and piling dirt into a steep barrier around the cultivated field. After the lands were properly surveyed and titles secured, fences were built. Mason did not always work his fields himself, however. In 1853 he lent Joseph Price $982.88 at five percent interest. As security, Price gave Mason three milk cows, three yoke of oxen and agreed to plant 100 acres of wheat and 60 acres of barley on land leased from Mason. Price promised not to harvest without permission from Wilson. If Price repaid the money on time, he got back the livestock and control of the grain crop; if not, Mason retained both. This was just one of many loans the Wilsons would make to their neighbors. Such private loans were common in those times, since there were no local banks yet.

The Wilsons continued to invest in real estate throughout the 1850s, even though the legal battle over the Vaca–Peña land grant was still being waged. Mason sold the first 200-acre parcel he had purchased, then steadily bought blocks of property in the townsite and more acreage surrounding the town plat on the west, south and east. It was not until 1856 that any of these deeds indicated caution about the land grant confirmation or any reference to professional surveys. Mason seemed to be gambling that the titles would be upheld, and eventually they were. By the end of 1859, Mason and Luzena owned most of the townsite, as well as 592 acres of surrounding land valued at $10 per acre, with improvements of $15,000 and about $13,000 in personal property. In eight years' time, the Wilsons had established themselves as one of the wealthiest families in Solano County.

Wilson's Hotel also received a major infusion of capital; a new two-story brick hotel was erected on the corner of Main and

Advertisements for stage lines and steam ships in the Weekly Solano Herald, *November 23, 1866. Solano County Archives.*

NEW LINE OF
DAILY STAGES!

THE Undersigned will hereafter run a Daily Line of Stages, carrying Passengers and Light Freights, between

VACAVILLE AND SUISUN!

Leaving VACAVILLE, on Monday, Wednesday and Friday, at 6 o'clock A. M., and reaching Suisun in time to connect with the steamer for San Francisco ; and on Tuesday, Thursday and Saturday, at 12 o'clock M., reaching Suisun in time to connect with Cutler's Stages for Benicia.

Returning -- will leave SUISUN, on Monday, Wednesday and Friday, at 2 o'clock P.M.; on Tuesday, Thursday and Saturday, on the arrival of the steamer from San Francisco.

Fare, each way - - $1.00.

☞ Express business, entrusted to the Driver, will be attended to with promptness and fidelity.

M. CUTLER, Proprietor.

Suisun, June 18th 1866—29tf

FOR SAN FRANCISCO.

THE COMMODIOUS

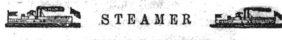 STEAMER

PAUL PRY,

A. D. CARPENTER..............Commander,

WILL RUN REGULARLY between SUISUN CITY and SAN FRANCISCO, touching at BENICIA and MARTINEZ, leaving Suisun every Monday, Wednesday and Friday, at 8 o'clock A. M.

RETURNING,

Will leave Pacific Street Wharf, San Francisco, every Tuesday, Thursday and Saturday morning, at 10 o'clock.

☞ For FREIGHT or PASSAGE, apply on board. tf

Receipt for a package containing $16 in coin shipped by W. J. Pleasants in 1866, signed by Mason Wilson, Wells Fargo agent. Vacaville Museum.

Davis Streets where the Walker Opera House now stands. A traveling correspondent for the *Sacramento Union* visited Vacaville in August 1858, providing a sketch of the little town along with good publicity for the Wilsons:

> *The land in the vicinity is entirely covered by Spanish grants, some of which . . . have been confirmed by the U.S. Supreme Court. A small portion—640 acres, and containing the village—was bought, some time ago, by Mason Wilson, from Vaca and Peña, the grantees. . . . The village is named after the first-named grantee, and not, as is vulgarly supposed, from the number of "cows" in the vicinity. . . . The village itself is fast increasing in permanent improvement. It contains one (too small) public house. A fine brick hotel is being built, (under the direction of Patton, architect, of Sacramento, by McCarty, contractor) by Wilson. There is a billiard room with two good tables, a Post Office, and several stores.[2]*

This billiard room may be the one where Luzena said men were "playing scientific games of billiards by firing at the balls with a pistol."

The new Wilson Hotel was completed in October 1858 at a cost of $14,000. The building was L-shaped, with the kitchen wing on the east end separate from the main part of the hotel to lessen the danger of fire, a common plan at the time. There were thirty guest rooms and a large dining room–parlor in the main wing which measured 30 by 65 feet. The other wing was 18 by 45 feet, and the kitchen 12 by 16 feet. The rooms were not very large by modern standards, but it was the most impressive structure on the Vacaville skyline at the time. To the east across a lane which is now Davis Street, was the barn, shaded by many eucalyptus. Willis Jepson, a Vacaville native son, said of the hotel:

> It was . . . substantial for its day, and everything about it bespoke solidity and the comfort of a first-class country inn. The horse stages from Vallejo stopped in front of the wide door that opened into a large traveler's room with a great fire-place on the east side and a resplendent bar in the southwest corner. From here a door led into a large well-appointed dining room whose windows looked out onto the spaces of a pleasant garden at the rear.[3]

Hester Allison, another early resident, remembered beautiful roses growing there. Drinking water came from a spring in nearby Ulatis Creek, which flowed year-round then. A little shed built over the water was used to cool and store milk from Luzena's beloved "mulley cow."[4]

Two years later another reporter passed through town and described the growth of the town:

> Mr. Wilson bought a tract of about 700 acres where the road crossed the creek, and on the bank of the creek built an inn. The place was a convenient one for travelers, on an important road, and soon there was a demand for a blacksmith shop, a store, a carpenter, a printer, etc., until at last the village came to have thirty buildings to it, all of them strung along the road which forms the only street.[5]

The arrival of the stagecoach was, according to Luzena, "the event of the day" in town; it was the link to the outside world. For the Wilsons, it was also a business contact since Mason was an agent for Wells Fargo & Company. He was listed in the *Pacific Coast Business Directory* of 1867 as both agent and hotel-keeper, so he probably operated the Wells Fargo office out of the hotel. Stages connected Vacaville to Napa, Luzena said, as well as Suisun; to get to San Francisco at that time, a traveler from Vacaville would go to Suisun, then board a steamer for the city. All this changed when the railroad arrived. Vacaville Stage Line charged 75 cents in July 1869, to carry passengers to the California Pacific Railroad depot five and a half miles away at Vaca Station, now called Elmira. Luzena remembered the old stagecoaches fondly, and bemoaned their eventual passing from the countryside. With the railroads, she believed, came "the aping of city airs and the following of city fashions."

Throughout her memoir, Luzena showed a strong interest in clothes and fashion. Arriving in Sacramento in 1849 wearing rags, she was embarrassed to encounter an acquaintance who was wearing a clean white shirt. She remembered her shame because "so much influence does clothing have on our feelings and intercourse with our fellow men." In Nevada City, her dress for the ball was ordinary calico, but it was clean and freshly ironed. She does not say if she bought herself a Chinese shawl, the ultimate feminine accessory then. The swirling skirts and colorful silk scarves of the señoritas dancing at the Vaca adobe pleased her, as did the elaborate jackets of the gentlemen. She was also delighted at the casual garb of the enthusiastic dancers who gathered in her Vacaville dining room for music and fun. So it would seem that in matters of dress, Luzena had completely forsaken Quaker plainness at age sixteen and never looked back. She enjoyed music, the theater, and dancing as well, all of which her Quaker ancestors would have condemned.

However, Luzena believed in working hard and maintaining high standards. She respected some of her neighbors, the "economical, industrious, energetic, thrifty families from the North and Canada." Conversely, she thought the immigrants from the southern and western states with their "shiftless ways" held back progress. This is an intriguing assessment, coming from a woman whose roots were in North Carolina and Missouri. Her story about "old Bob" the cat is told with her usual dry humor, but her disapproval of slovenly housekeeping is obvious. Willis Jepson, always blunt in his opinions, had a slightly different perspective.

> The energy and native capacity of Mrs. Wilson was so great that perhaps it is natural we find her deriding shiftless neighbors. The whole of Vaca Valley and the neighboring valleys were settled mainly by Southerners—families from Virginia, Kentucky and especially Missouri. The Missourians have long been considered fair game for derision and banter. Unquestionably the Yankees are much "smarter," but relatively as many or more Missourians in Vaca Valley held on to their ranches during the panic years . . . as did Yankees. The men of the valley who have defrauded their neighbors, however, in the grand Stanford–Huntington manner, have all been Yankees with the exception of one Southerner.

Luzena's strong spirit of enterprise undoubtedly developed in her early years among the Quakers and formed her character for life. Wherever she went, she understood the necessity for work and the importance of community in promoting the common good. Independent yet neighborly, gracious yet disciplined, Luzena was perfectly suited to her role as a pioneer. The strength that sustained her through her early days would be needed again, for her troubles were by no means over.

NOTES

1. *San Francisco Chronicle,* January 9, 1910, 4.
2. *Alta California,* August 13, 1858, 1.
3. Unpublished letter from Willis Jepson to Francis Farquhar, March 21, 1939. See Appendix II.
4. Luther Harbison letter, June 14, 1918.
5. *Alta California,* July 17, 1860, 2.

Jubilant passengers and a proud crew pose aboard the first Vaca Valley Railroad train to reach the town of Winters in August 1875. This northerly extension of the railway put Winters on the map and brought prosperity to the region's ranchers by connecting them directly with their markets via Vaca Station. Mason Wilson was one of the founders of this railroad. Lavinia Young in memory of Robert Young.

22

W ITH THE MEXICAN LAND GRANT ISSUE SETTLED, Vacaville grew from a village into a town. Mason began to sell lots in the town plat, granting deeds to more than thirty buyers in the 1860s. Prices ranged between $100 and $2,300, depending on the size of the lot and its location. Main Street lots with commercial potential were the most expensive, of course. The early deeds bore only Mason's name, but gradually Luzena's name began to appear as co-grantor. At the end of each recorded deed, the county clerk routinely confirmed the identity of the parties executing the deed and verified that he or she was doing so freely. However, if Luzena's name was recorded, he interviewed Luzena alone and added the following language:

> *And the said Luzena S. Wilson, wife of the said Mason Wilson, having by me first made acquainted with the contents of said instrument, acknowledged to me on examination apart from and without the hearing of her husband, that she executed the same freely and voluntarily without fear or compulsion or undue influence of her husband and that she did not wish to retract the execution of the same.*[1]

Thus were her rights preserved under the California State Constitution, which granted married women the right to own property.

In one early real estate transaction, the Wilsons and Professor Anderson sold the Ulatis Academy, its land and buildings, to the Methodist Episcopal Church, South, and thus the Pacific Methodist College was launched in 1861. Although named a college, the school actually functioned as a combination high school and elementary school. There was a distinct need for higher education in California; as late as 1865, California had only six public schools for secondary education. The gap was filled by private entrepreneurs such as Professor Anderson or by church-sponsored institutions. Children could enroll in Pacific Methodist College in the primary or preparatory programs, as long as their families could afford the tuition. Upper grade students came from all over Northern California, and enrollment reached 190 pupils just two years after the college opened its doors.

The Methodist College lasted only ten years in Vacaville, but it served the community and the Wilson family well. Luzena's second son, Jay Crittenden Wilson, graduated from the school in 1865, and both Mason Jr. and Correnah were students there. Mason Wilson Sr. was a solid supporter, serving as a trustee and playing a vital role in assisting the college in its recovery from a fire that destroyed the building in April 1865. The fire was probably the work of an arsonist angered by the assassination of President Lincoln. There was much sympathy for the Southern cause in the Vaca Valley, but there was strong Union support as well. The college took no sides in the conflict, but since the sponsoring church was identified with the Southern Methodists, the school became a target. Mason helped organize the effort to start a building fund, and by the next year a new brick structure was finished. It was in a new location, however, on a hilltop on the north side of Ulatis Creek. Mason traded property with the college, giving them a prime location in what is now known as Andrews Park. This second college building changed hands several times over the next thirty years, and was torn down in 1895 after it was weakened by earthquake. But while it lasted, it was a community landmark and a source of civic pride.

The public record shows the Wilsons were active promoters of the college, but not everyone viewed them as model citizens. Willis Jepson, born too late to have known the college himself, voiced opinions he probably heard from his mother Martha. Jepson said the Wilsons were neither progressive nor civic-minded; "they cared only for the interests of the Wilsons and for their interests narrowly." Jepson castigated them for refusing to sell choice town lots to fine families who wanted to locate near the college. He claimed the Wilson would only part with unattractive, poor lots further away from town, thus effectively driving away these cultured citizens from Vacaville and weakening the college. Unfortunately for Jepson, available land records do not support his claims. The Wilsons sold numerous lots along Main Street and opposite the college during the 1860s, and they never owned the arid land in question. His bitter comments hint that some people in the valley may have resented the Wilsons, their power or their wealth. Possibly Mason and Luzena did drive a hard bargain in business; ill will can easily arise between neighbors in a small town over real or perceived grievances.

Fiery Passions of the Civil War

ONE AUGUST MORNING, when I was about five years old, my father took me with him into Vacaville. It must have been the year 1872. The village main street, one short block long, had only a few scattered stores and shops on its south side, a livery stable, a drug store and a residence on the north side. Each store had a porch or platform in front, set above the general level of the roadway with one or two steps leading up to the platform.

On this August morning a little crowd of men had gathered under the shade of the trees which lined the village street—farmers from the countryside, cattle drivers from Suisun, a sprinkling of ranch laborers, a few teamsters from Maine Prairie, one or two hunters from the back hills, the blacksmith, the shoemaker, and the two doctors of the village. All were intently listening to a fiery orator who, in the presidential campaign of that year, was loudly denouncing General Ulysses S. Grant, the Republican nominee for President, and as loudly extolling the virtues and honors of his opponent, Horace Greeley, the Democratic nominee. The speaker heaped upon Grant the most virulent abuse; he breathed fire and brimstone and ridiculed all claims made in his behalf that he was a general. From beginning to end, from Bull Run to Appomattox, he fought the Civil War battles over again. Once in a while he would stop and appeal to a little man who sat on the platform steps. This little man had small features, a short thin fuzz of a beard on this chin, and was called Bush Stevenson. In his hands was a book, whose pages he busily turned and supplied the orator with the losses in Civil War battles. The figures given were always against General Grant and in favor of General McClellan and other generals.

Across the vacant lots between the stores the golden wheat fields, only three hundred yards away, glowed in the white-hot sunshine and over the straight treeless level of the valley floor beyond rose the oak-dotted range of little hills of that ranch which so many years later Elise P. Buckingham named Araquipa—the land of peace. But on that August day no one in the village street regarded that scene of serene and quiet beauty. All eyes were held as if fascinated by the ardent and fluent orator who roused deeply and adroitly every Civil War enmity.

It is not within my remembrance, when very young, that I feared bulls, badgers or bats, but my whole nature was deeply terrified by men whose dark and gloomy passions found vent in stirring the smouldering hatreds of the American Civil War.

—Willis Linn Jepson, *Vacaville Reporter,* May 12, 1945.

Young Willis Linn Jepson. Like many early Vacaville residents, the Jepsons were Southern sympathizers. Willis thought that "the fires of our Civil War will die slowly because certain problems in the social order were not settled by it. Possibly they can never be settled." Vacaville Heritage Council.

The politics of the Civil War were another source of tension in the daily lives of the townsfolk. Hester Allison, daughter of pioneer Josiah Allison, recalled:

> *My father often told me about the election of 1860. He and Mason Wilson were two of the four men in Vacaville who had the moral courage to vote for Abraham Lincoln. There was no such thing as a secret ballot then. The men stood in line and, literally, shouted to the clerk their choice of candidates. The town was seething with Southern sympathizers, and my father and the other three men didn't really know what to expect from the crowd. The feeling was running very high.[2]*

Emotion over the war was probably intense in the Wilson household when Thomas accepted an appointment to the U.S. Naval Academy. He left home in 1862 to serve his country and the Union cause. If Luzena's Quaker background caused her any qualms about her son's enlistment, she left no public record of them. Mason, for his part, remained a lifelong Republican.

In spite of the turbulence of the Civil War years, prosperity had finally come to the Wilsons. Hester Allison described Mason as "the wealthiest man in the town."[3] The Hotel was well established and the gamble the Wilsons had taken in

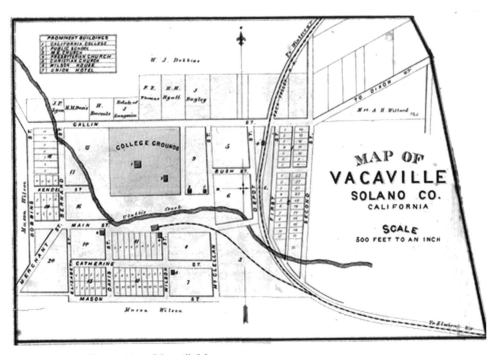

Downtown Vacaville circa 1877. Vacaville Museum.

buying land in the early years was paying off handsomely. A local newspaper each year announced the top "nabobs" of the county, based upon the assessed value of land and property; Mason Wilson regularly made the list.

With his financial position secure, Mason took a prominent role in community affairs. In the town's earliest days, he lobbied to have Vacaville chosen as the county seat, and he joined the Society of California Pioneers in 1869. When Vacaville citizens formed the Vaca Valley Railroad that year to connect to the newly-completed railroad line at Vaca Station, Mason was elected president of the company. This fledgling rail line was launched with high hopes of linking Vacaville to the fertile and productive lands to the north in Lake and Yolo counties. But within three months, Mason was replaced as president; the company continued under the leadership of the two Stevenson brothers but never reached the potential envisioned by the early founders.

At about this time, Mason seemed restless. He took a trip to Texas on a steamship in early 1867 when he was sixty years old. Impressed with the possibilities there, he returned and tried to sell his Vacaville property in order to relocate, but he was not successful. Melissa Allison wrote in 1871:

> *Mr. Wilson made a desperate effort all fall and winter to sell his place and go back to Texas. But he could not sell and I believe has given up going. He is going into the grape business largely.*[4]

Why was he unable to sell? Perhaps Luzena opposed the sale and would not sign the deeds. After achieving relative comfort and stability in California, she may not have wanted to start over in Texas. It is possible that no one could afford to buy him out, a disadvantage of being the richest man in town. Or maybe he was undergoing a personal crisis; subsequent events seem to support this last theory. In December 1872, Mason abruptly left his family and everyone seemed stunned. The newspaper headline read:

> UNACCOUNTABLE AFFAIR: *On Wednesday of last week, Mason Wilson, one of the oldest, wealthiest, best known and most highly respected citizens of Vacaville, left home to go to Dixon on business, telling his wife that he might be gone all night. He remained away all night, and the next morning Mrs. Wilson, instead of greeting her husband as she expected, received a letter from him, written at Dixon, informing her that she would probably never see him again; that all he had was hers during her lifetime, but that he wished it to go to their two youngest children at her death. Since then, it has been ascertained that on the day he left home he was in Sacramento endeavoring to purchase $500 in greenbacks, but no further trace of him has been found. As he was known not to be*

embarrassed financially (owning unencumbered property to the value of $75,000 with $9,000 on deposit in Sacramento); as he was happy in his domestic relations, and as he was in robust health, there is no assignable cause for this strange freak of a hitherto staid and sober citizen.[5]

At fifty-three, Luzena found herself alone, abandoned by her husband a few days before their twenty-eighth wedding anniversary. Mason probably boarded the newly finished transcontinental railroad in Sacramento, traveling east to Missouri, the state where he and Luzena had met. The trip to St. Joseph would have taken five days. A few weeks later a Solano County newspaper printed a follow up story with this blunt assessment:

Mason Wilson has been heard from. He was in southwestern Missouri, and intimates that the reason for his leaving here was that there was a plan on foot for sending him to the Asylum at Stockton; which is conclusive evidence that he was a fit subject for that institution.[6]

The insanity theory was bolstered by another newspaper report:

A. M. Stevenson informs us that he is in receipt of a letter from Dallas, Texas under date of January 7 saying that Mason Wilson, of Vacaville, was in that place, and the writer thought that he exhibited evidences of insanity. The writer also said that he had facilities for keeping track of him, and would do so until further advised.[7]

The anonymous letter writer may have been Jay, then age twenty-four, who did indeed go to Texas to live with his father. Evidently Luzena never saw her husband again, and no further public explanation of his sudden departure was ever made known. The mental illness theory may have been generally accepted, but Willis Jepson, ever the contrarian, had another theory.

Luzena, Forty-niner, was a determined and strong-minded personage—a woman of the real pioneer type. But even so her husband, Mason Wilson, became wearied. He could stand Luzena no longer and he went away from Vaca Valley. He . . . put as much distance between himself and Luzena as he well could.

Since young Jepson was only five years old when Mason decamped, he was again repeating things he heard from others; his views on Mason's state of mind could be gossip, gospel-truth, or a little of both. Whatever the reason, Mason's departure was probably not unduly shocking to California society. After all, the state was well-populated with men who had previously abandoned home and family to make a new life in the West.

In spite of the rift in the marriage, the family business continued in an orderly manner. Within a few months, Mason appeared before a magistrate in McLennan County, Texas, and gave Luzena full power of attorney over all his property and assets in California.[8] Jay apparently maintained his relationship with his mother, while continuing to provide for his father's welfare. Thomas helped Luzena adjust to her new reality. Luzena seemed to maintain silence on the subject of her husband; she never mentioned him by name in her entire memoir. In the stories where he did appear, she was proud of his work ethic, commended his bravery, and told of the jokes and hardships they shared. Nonetheless, Mason remains a shadowy figure, his personality and motivations largely unknown.

During her years alone, business affairs became Luzena's primary focus. When Mason left, they owned 600 acres of farmland which she continued to work. Like other area farmers, she began to plant fruit orchards instead of grain crops. She owned the usual farm equipment such as wagons and tools. Her inventory of livestock in 1873 was impressive: 100 horses, 6 colts, 4 mules, 7 cows, 9 cattle, 2 cashmere goats, 58 goats, and 30 hogs. The next year she added 600 sheep to the list. The goats were pastured on a hill near town which was appropriately-called Goat Hill. The top of that hill today is the intersection of Mason and Wilson Streets.

Sales of town lots continued steadily and provided a comfortable income. Luzena managed the Wilson Hotel until 1874 when she sold it to Ike Davis for the considerable sum of $6,000 in gold coin. She was also in the business of loaning out money and holding mortgages at the going rate of twelve percent interest. The list of prominent men who borrowed from her includes L. W. Buck and William Cantelow, names well known in Vacaville even today. She made new loans and also handled the $7,900 in mortgages and loans that were outstanding when Mason departed. Most of these loans were secured by real estate.

With Thomas as her estate manager, Luzena made the transition to life on her own. By 1875, her family seemed well settled. Mason Jr. had moved to San Francisco to work as a clerk in a brokerage office, and Correnah had graduated from Mills Seminary and was at home again. Jay was still in Texas. Luzena was comfortable enough to enjoy traveling, and in June 1877, she and Correnah took a vacation to Yosemite. They came home to ashes and disaster.

The fire started in her own barn. Thomas had just put his horse away and locked the barn after returning from Suisun. He went into the house and was attending to correspondence when he heard the shouts of alarm. He ran outside, found the barn in flames and the wind carrying the fire to the blacksmith's shop next door. The village had no fire department, and the spreading flames rapidly burned nearly half the buildings in town, including many businesses. Luzena suffered heavy losses. Her house was gone with all her possessions and furniture, including her precious square grand piano, the first Steinway piano in Solano County. She carried no insurance on the house, but the barn and the hay in it were insured for $1,000—only a fraction of their true worth. Two of her other buildings which burned were also uninsured. The cause of the fire was never determined, though many suspected hobos or gypsies might have set it.

On a windy day one week later, one of her wheat fields was set afire by a spark thrown from a passing Vaca Valley railway train. She lost 100 acres of standing wheat; two adjoining properties also burned, destroying some harvested grain and a lot of fencing. She and the other growers had to sue for compensation, which they finally received. As the newspaper commiserated, "Misfortunes seldom come singly."[9] Subsequent events would prove this statement prophetic.

When Luzena's wheat field burned, she may have counted it a mixed blessing. Although wheat was the principal crop grown in Vaca Valley in early days, by 1877 it was not very profitable. She got compensation for the crop and also saved the expense of hiring a harvesting crew like this one pictured on a Haines harvester. Grain fields were rapidly replaced by orchards. One Vaca Valley grower calculated that in 1880, fifteen mature pear trees yielded more profit than his 1,900 acres of wheat. Vacaville Heritage Council.

A third fire erupted in October, just as Vacaville's 350 residents had begun to make progress in rebuilding after the destruction four months earlier. This time the entire downtown business district was lost except for the Davis Hotel, the brick building the Wilsons had built in 1858. Luzena lost two more small houses, both uninsured. Many businesses vowed to build yet again but others closed up permanently. Arson was suspected once again, but no one was ever brought to justice.

Left with no home and few worldly goods, Luzena soon decided to leave town. In her memoir, she said the Vaca Valley had been her home for twenty-seven years which dates her departure at 1878, a few months after the series of fires. At this time, Mason Jr. was living at 1546 Howard Street in San Francisco, and Luzena, Thomas and Correnah joined him there. Luzena would maintain close ties to friends in Vacaville, celebrate the town's rebirth and growth, and remain prominent in its business affairs, but she would live the rest of her days as a San Franciscan.

NOTES

1. Solano County, Recorder of Deeds, Book F 1, Page 101.
2. *Vacaville Reporter,* October 15, 1948, 2.
3. Hester Allison Harbison's handwritten footnotes on copy of "Prunings from Vaca Valley," Allison Collection, Vacaville Museum.
4. Melissa Allison's letter, March 7, 1871, Allison Collection, Vacaville Museum.
5. *Weekly Solano Republican,* December 12, 1872, 2.
6. *Weekly Solano Republican,* January 16, 1872, 2. Coincidentally, the Stockton asylum was known to Luzena through a family connection. Jennie Day Hunt, the wife of Luzena's brother William Gaston Hunt, was the daughter of the general contractor who built the institution.
7. *Weekly Solano Republican,* January 23, 1873, 3.
8. Solano County Abstract Company File No. 249, 49. Unpublished document, Vacaville Museum.
9. *Weekly Solano Republican,* June 15, 1877, 3.

Correnah and Luzena in the 1880s, probably in one of their San Francisco residences. Mills College Alumnae Association.

L UZENA'S EARLY DAYS IN THE CITY were not entirely trouble-free. Correnah, then twenty-three years old, fell seriously ill during the winter of
1880–1881 and her recovery was slow. Fortunately, she and Luzena used
their time well; Correnah carefully recorded her mother's stories of the pioneer
days. The two women must have been proud of their work since they soon
agreed to have it published as a series in the *Argonaut,* a San Francisco newspaper.
Ten issues of the paper between February and April 1881 carried an installment
of Luzena's memoir. However, readers never knew the author's identity, since
each column was simply signed "W." Later, Correnah donated the bound, type-
written manuscript to Mills College which has preserved it. Burned into the
leather covering the volume is the title used in the *Argonaut:* "A Woman's Reminiscences of Early Days." Both Correnah and Luzena signed the final page.
Although she claimed to have recorded her mother's words accurately, Correnah probably did extensive editing. Willis Jepson certainly thought so:

> *We may be sure her [Luzena's] thoughts would have been expressive and forceful,*
> *although the telling diction and polished sentences would have been no other than those*
> *of her daughter Corrhena [sic], alumna of Mills College, because Mrs. Wilson, with all*
> *her many virtues, was still an uneducated and rugged pioneer.*

Jepson was well-educated and qualified to comment; he had earned a Ph.D. and
was a distinguished professor of botany at University of California at Berkeley.
 The next fall, Luzena learned that she was a widow. Mason Wilson Sr. died
September 5, 1882. He spent the last ten years of his life in Texas, but details of
his life there are sketchy. After leaving Vacaville, he settled south of Waco in
Moody, Texas, where farming and livestock formed the economic base. He had

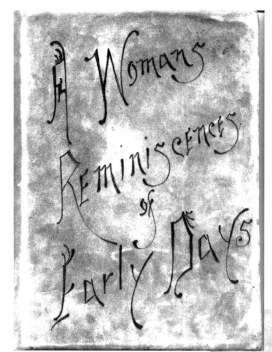

Left: Correnah prepared the original type-written manuscript of her mother's memoir, which she donated to her alma mater, Mills College. The pages were bound in a book with a leather cover. Correnah probably designed and executed the pyrographic cover art.

Below: The final page is signed by both women. Special Collections, F. W. Olin Library, Mills College.

first bought Texas land in October 1870, while he was in California trying to sell his holdings there, and he continued to accumulate real estate. But in 1879, Mason deeded all his Texas holdings to Jay, who had recently married. Mason lived with his son's family long enough to meet his first grandson, Asa Cohen Wilson, born in early 1880. Enigmatic to the end of his days, Mason was buried in the Naler Cemetery in Moody, Texas.

Mason had made a will in 1867, leaving everything to Luzena, his "beloved wife," so the probate process moved smoothly for her. The appraised value of the estate was set at $23,550, the largest single asset being a 170-acre parcel of land.[1] Ten years earlier Luzena and Mason owned more than 600 acres in Solano County; so obviously, Luzena had been selling off property. There were many

The Hotel Pleasanton at the northwest corner of Sutter and Jones in San Francisco was Luzena's home during her last fourteen years. San Francisco History Center, San Francisco Public Library.

transactions, both small and large, during that decade. For example, four months before Mason's death, Luzena sold 492 acres to William Parker of Vacaville for $61,500. The acreage included most of the Wilson land to the east of the town proper, as well as a large parcel south and west of town. Parker laid out lots and petitioned to expand the town boundaries to embrace "Parker's Addition." Her next major deal was even more lucrative. In 1887, the Buck brothers paid $88,560 for 148 acres, comprising the land to the west of town and north of the land Parker bought earlier. Buck's Addition to Vacaville soon followed.

Even after these impressive transactions, Luzena still owned numerous blocks of town property and their sales yielded a reliable, though more modest, income. Luzena gave Thomas power of attorney in early 1883, and he managed all her real estate holdings and financial matters from that point onward. Not to be out-done by the Bucks and Parker, Thomas laid out Wilson's Addition to Vacaville in 1895.

With Thomas now handling the business, Luzena traveled more, embarking on a year-long tour of Europe with Correnah in 1883. She never forgot her roots in the soil of Vaca Valley, however, and on an excursion to the continent eight years later, she collected grape cuttings and brought them to Vacaville. The grow-ers who planted them named the fruit Luzena grapes in her honor.[2] She explored California as well; Mr. Rush, a rancher from Fairfield, recalled encountering Thomas and Luzena in 1897 in a Los Angeles hotel where they were vacationing.

Before Correnah's marriage in 1886, Luzena lived with her daughter in sever-al different San Francisco dwellings. By 1888, she and son Thomas had established their residence in the Hotel Pleasanton, a self-described "Family and Tourist Hotel." The rates were reasonable, $2 to $3.50 per day, and many peo-ple chose to live in hotels rather than maintain a private home. For Luzena, it was perhaps a fitting luxury—after so many years of operating a hotel, she undoubt-edly enjoyed good service and convenience as a guest. Luzena was a permanent resident there for fourteen years. In the 1888 *San Francisco Blue Book,* "The Fash-ionable Private Address Directory and Ladies' Visiting and Shopping Guide," Luzena announced that she was at home to callers on Monday.

The only known photograph of Luzena dates to these days in San Francisco. She appears as a well-dressed Victorian lady, having tea with Correnah. Seated at a table, she looks into the camera, poised and content. In her face there is strength and in her bearing, confidence.

She may have briefly considered moving back to Solano County. After return-ing from her first trip to Europe, she visited the Vaca Valley in May 1884. The newspaper reported:

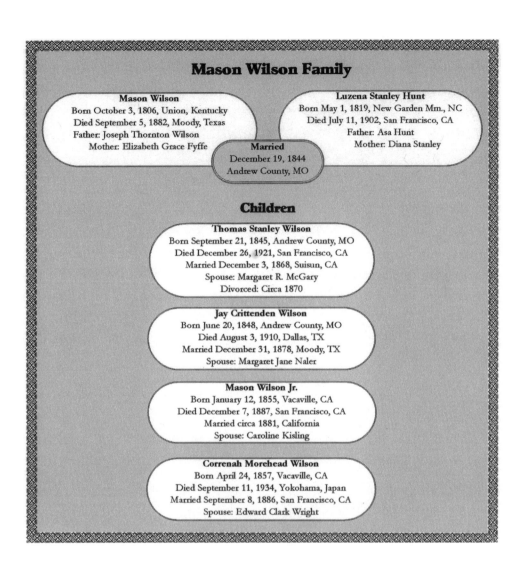

Mason Wilson Family

Mason Wilson
Born October 3, 1806, Union, Kentucky
Died September 5, 1882, Moody, Texas
Father: Joseph Thornton Wilson
Mother: Elizabeth Grace Fyffe

Luzena Stanley Hunt
Born May 1, 1819, New Garden Mm., NC
Died July 11, 1902, San Francisco, CA
Father: Asa Hunt
Mother: Diana Stanley

Married
December 19, 1844
Andrew County, MO

Children

Thomas Stanley Wilson
Born September 21, 1845, Andrew County, MO
Died December 26, 1921, San Francisco, CA
Married December 3, 1868, Suisun, CA
Spouse: Margaret R. McGary
Divorced: Circa 1870

Jay Crittenden Wilson
Born June 20, 1848, Andrew County, MO
Died August 3, 1910, Dallas, TX
Married December 31, 1878, Moody, TX
Spouse: Margaret Jane Naler

Mason Wilson Jr.
Born January 12, 1855, Vacaville, CA
Died December 7, 1887, San Francisco, CA
Married circa 1881, California
Spouse: Caroline Kisling

Correnah Morehead Wilson
Born April 24, 1857, Vacaville, CA
Died September 11, 1934, Yokohama, Japan
Married September 8, 1886, San Francisco, CA
Spouse: Edward Clark Wright

Mrs. Luzena S. Wilson arrived in Vacaville Monday, and was warmly greeted by her hosts of friends. It is her intention to establish her future home here and [she] will shortly commence the erection of a magnificent residence.[3]

Her name was listed in the Solano County business directory that year where she was identified as a carpet weaver. She built no mansions in Vacaville, however, nor was there any further reference to carpet-making. When she came to town, she was known to stay at the Davis House, her old home.

Another major tragedy befell her late in 1887, when Mason Wilson Jr. died after a long illness. He left a wife and a five-year-old son who was also named

Mason. Mason Jr. was living in San Francisco at the time of his death, and the family was together to support one another in that sad time. In addition to her three surviving children, Luzena's family then included three grandchildren: Asa Cohen Wilson and Rowena Wilson, ages seven and three, living in Texas with their parents, Jay and Margaret; and Mason Kisling Wilson, living with his newly-widowed mother, Caroline.

Luzena's interest in business continued under Thomas's management. Her portfolio expanded to include some railroad bonds, and she continued to make private loans secured by property. She bought land in Yolo County and San Francisco, but the extent of her holdings in the city cannot be fully ascertained, since many records were destroyed by the fire and earthquake of 1906. However, she owned a lot on the south side of Geary Street, between Mason and Powell, which the family sold in 1912.

Luzena's last known visit to Vacaville was in November 1901. She and Thomas stayed at the Hotel Raleigh, and the *Vacaville Reporter* duly noted her presence:

> *Mrs. Wilson has not visited Vacaville for several years and expresses surprise at the splendid growth it has made since her last visit. She was one of the earliest settlers, coming here in 1851.[4]*

The following summer, the same newspaper printed her obituary. Luzena Stanley Wilson died July 11, 1902, at the Hotel Pleasanton; she lived a full 83 years, 2 months and 10 days. Death was caused by thyroid cancer, with senility a pre-existing condition. The funeral was held at Correnah's home and burial was handled by the International Order of Odd Fellows Crematory, where a private interment ceremony laid her to rest at Greenlawn Memorial Park in Colma. In her will, of which only a fragment has survived, she left her entire estate to her three surviving children, Thomas, Jay and Correnah. Nothing is known of her personal bequests, so there are no clues to her relationships with her three grand-children and her widowed daughter-in-law.

One hundred years after her death, Luzena Stanley Wilson remains a fascinating character. She overcame many hardships and kept her sense of humor. She valued friendship and genuinely enjoyed the variety of people she encountered during her long life. Her courage was tested repeatedly, and though she may have bent under the strain, she never broke down. The source of this inner strength surely had its roots in her Quaker family life, where independent thought was encouraged while outward conformity was required. Though she left the Quakers early in life, her character was shaped by her early training which taught her the equality of women, a true work ethic, honesty and community-mindedness.

Her children eulogized her as a devoted "beloved mother."[5] Such an epitaph would probably have pleased her. So, a glimpse into the fates of Thomas, Jay, Mason Jr. and Correnah will provide a fitting memorial to their mother and will complete the portrait of this pioneer woman.

NOTES

1. Probate File No. 712, Solano County Archives, Fairfield, California.
2. *Vacaville Reporter,* April 15, 1974, 8.
3. *Vacaville Reporter,* May 17, 1884, 4.
4. *Vacaville Reporter,* November 2, 1901, 5.
5. *San Francisco Daily Call,* July 13, 1902, 36.

Thomas Stanley Wilson circa 1865. United States Navy.

THOMAS STANLEY WILSON CELEBRATED HIS FOURTH BIRTHDAY September 21, 1849, just as his family reached Sacramento. His welcoming committee was exclusively male, and the homesick miners and immigrants passed Thomas and his brother Jay around the campfire like sleeping treasures. Though born in Missouri, Thomas would claim California as his home throughout his seventy-six years.

His early boyhood was spent in the village of Vacaville; he was 5½ years old when the Wilson family arrived there. Luzena mentioned that her boys played as "squatters" and "settlers" and recalled their horseback trip together to the Wolfskills. A boy in early California quite likely kept busy learning to ride, hunt, climb, fish and roam. There were no Indians to fear, since most of the native Patwins had vanished from the area by 1840 because of diseases such as smallpox and forced relocation to the Spanish Missions. The few who remained in the region worked on the ranchos. There were some hazards such as wild animals and accidents, but a youngster with few chores was living in a natural paradise.

The confines of the classroom may have come as a bit of a shock. Thomas started his studies in the canvas schoolhouse Luzena described, but by age eleven he was enrolled in Ulatis Academy under the capable instruction of Professor Anderson. Luckily, the professor's standards were high and Thomas received a quality education which prepared him well.

At age 16½, Thomas reported to the U. S. Naval Academy in Newport, Rhode Island. The Academy had moved there from Annapolis the previous year and remained in Newport for the duration of the Civil War. Young men who wanted to attend the academy were usually nominated by their congressional representatives, with final appointment contingent upon passing a physical and academic exam. Representative Aaron A. Sargent, a Nevada City resident in 1850 when the Wilsons were there, was representing the Wilsons' district in 1861 and he secured Thomas' appointment. New midshipmen were normally nominated in the spring and started their studies in the fall. Thomas, however, entered in May 1862. He was the only man from California, and perhaps his late arrival was due to the distance he had to travel.

Thomas did well in his studies. During his first year, he ranked nineteenth in a class of thirty-three; solidly in the middle. He excelled in geometry, trigonometry and mechanics, but his marks in seamanship and infantry tactics were average. Two months at sea on the practice ship were also included in this year's curriculum. In his second and final year, he spent more than five months at sea and improved his marks in both seamanship and gunnery. He continued to shine in science and math, earning top grades in astronomy, physics, mechanics and navigation. At his graduation in November 1864, he was honored as one of the five top midshipmen in his class. The course of instruction was usually four years in length, not two; but wartime dictated speed, and Thomas and his classmates were on the fast track.

After graduation, Thomas was assigned to the *U.S.S. Vermont,* which served as a receiving ship at the New York Naval Yard in Brooklyn. It appears Thomas spent his entire Naval career attached to this ship and awaiting orders, according to a pension form he completed in 1891. Various newspaper sketches in Vacaville and San Francisco over the years stated that Thomas was on an ironclad vessel on the Mississippi and was wounded during the battle at Vicksburg. Another article claimed he was involved in the naval blockade of the South that the Union Navy operated out of Port Royal. Both Vicksburg and the Port Royal blockade were pivotal Civil War naval engagements, and a veteran of either would merit a certain aura of respect and glory, but there is no evidence to support either story. The battle for Vicksburg occurred May through July 1863, and the ironclads indeed played a vital role in the Union victory there. Thomas was still in the Academy, however, training on the practice ship; seasoned sailors filled the positions on the front lines, manning the newly manufactured ironclads. As for Port Royal, it is certain that the *U.S.S. Vermont* was there from March 1862 until August 1864. She was a flagship, store ship, a receiving and ordnance supply vessel, and also served as a hospital. She departed for New York in 1864 after completing her mission in Port Royal. The newly-graduated Thomas joined her crew there at the Brooklyn Naval Yard. Perhaps excessive hometown pride led the local newspaper to inflate Thomas' wartime record to include a touch of heroism, or Thomas himself may have made the claim.

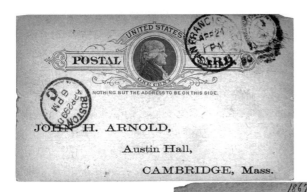

Harvard Law School alumni were listed in a directory which was published every five years. Written in his own hand, Thomas' postcard responses noted his various careers: farmer, lawyer and ultimately, capitalist. Special Collections, Harvard Law School Library.

Thomas resigned from the Navy in August 1865, citing nearsightedness as his reason for leaving. There may have been other factors as well: the war was over, Lincoln was dead, and perhaps young Wilson did not see a future for himself in a peacetime Navy. It is interesting to note that twenty-five years later he applied to the U.S. government for a pension, claiming his eye disease had its onset during his years in the Naval Academy and caused his resignation. The examining doctors did not find his vision abnormal or his eyes diseased; his claim was denied, and he was declared ineligible for the monthly pension of $6 to $12 offered by Congress. But this rejected pension application contains the only known physical description of Thomas. The doctor described him as "well nourished," six feet tall and weighing 200 pounds at age forty-five. Thomas wore glasses, but had no other physical defects or impairment, and he claimed no war wounds.

With his Naval career at an end, Thomas set his sights on Harvard Law School, which he entered September 9, 1865, one month after leaving the Navy. He graduated in two years with an LL.B., a Bachelor of Laws degree. Armed with these impressive credentials, he returned to California and took up the practice of law in San Francisco at the office of John B. Felton, Esquire. Thomas later set up his own office on Clay Street while he lived on Third Street.

Once established, his thoughts turned to matrimony. His chosen bride was Margaret Raymond McGary, known to her family as Maggie. The McGary family had settled in the Vaca Valley in the 1850s along with the Wilsons, and there was a close friendship between the two families. Maggie was one month younger

Tom Wilson planted Bartlett pears, peaches, French prunes and grapes on the Wilson land east of Vacaville in the early 1880s. In laying out the trees and vines he was clearly planning for future subdivision since each small section of land contained a variety of each crop. The dirt lane through the orchard is now Buck Avenue. The rooftops of the town are visible on the eastern horizon. S. M. Dobbins Collection, Vacaville Museum.

than Thomas and the two had gone to school together in the early days before the McGarys moved away. An astute businessman, Edward McGary moved his family to Cordelia, west of Fairfield, California, where he bought considerable property. Given such a long acquaintance and with both families favorably inclined, prospects for the marriage seemed highly favorable. Since she was Catholic and Thomas was not, Maggie had to obtain a special dispensation from Reverend Joseph Alemany of the Archdiocese of San Francisco. With permission granted, the ceremony took place December 3, 1868 at the McGary home. Mr. and Mrs. Thomas Wilson settled in San Francisco.

Late that year, silver was discovered in White Pine, Nevada, near the town of Hamilton. The newspapers were full of exciting stories about the "New El Dorado" and men were flocking there in great numbers. New towns sprang up overnight in Lander County, Nevada, and rumors spread rapidly as well. Thomas lost no time in heading out, presumably leaving his new bride behind. While he was in Hamilton in January 1869, word came that his congressman, James A. Johnson, had recommended him for a diplomatic post. Frederick Seward, Assistant Secretary of State to President Andrew Johnson, was considering Thomas for the job of Consul at Copenhagen, Denmark. This dazzling news was misreported in the local newspaper; they wrote that Thomas had been nominated by the President, not recommended to him. In the end, nothing came of it, and someone else was appointed.

Good wishes and bright prospects were not enough to ensure marital bliss for Thomas and his bride. Scarcely two years passed before Maggie was back living with her parents; the couple divorced, and no reason was cited publicly. Differences in religion or politics may have been factors, since the Wilsons were Republicans and the McGarys were active Democrats. Even the local newspaper took note of Thomas and his father-in-law's opposing positions in local political matters. Maggie eventually remarried and had three children by her second husband, Samuel Poorman.

Shortly after the divorce, Thomas' father left Vacaville for Texas. Thomas, now twenty-seven years old, came to assist Luzena in managing the farm lands and real estate holdings, and remained close to his mother until her death. He lived with her in Vacaville until the fires in 1877 destroyed their home, then moved with Luzena and Correnah to San Francisco. He claimed Vacaville as his principal residence for two more decades but his time was divided between his rural home and the city. He kept a law office in San Francisco although he never resumed an active legal career. After Correnah's marriage, Thomas and Luzena lived at the Hotel Pleasanton on the corner of Sutter and Jones streets.

In 1883, Luzena granted Thomas power of attorney over all her business affairs, an act which signaled her retirement from hands-on involvement. Thomas was a visible and active member of the Vacaville community. He was elected a director of the California Normal and Scientific School which opened in Vacaville in 1884. As a representative of the Masonic Lodge, he assisted in laying the cornerstone for the school's new building in October of that year. The local newspaper, the *Vacaville Reporter,* noted his comings and goings, his real estate transactions, and capital improvements on his properties. Since the Wilson estate encompassed most of the town, Vacaville's growth was directly linked to the Wilsons' plans. The *Reporter* observed that "T. S. Wilson keeps on steadily removing the ancient landmarks and extending his boundary lines so that Vacaville may go west and 'grow with the country.'"[1] Rumors also were floated about his political career, including speculation that he might run for governor or the U.S. Senate on the Republican ticket!

Throughout the decades of the 1880s and 1890s Thomas continued the farming operations, and listed his occupation as farmer on his Harvard alumni questionnaires and in the U.S. census. He grew grain crops, especially barley and wheat, and later added orchard and vine crops. He apparently was a gentleman farmer, providing housing for his field hands who did all the manual labor.

He was regarded as one of Vacaville's favorite sons, even after he made San Francisco his official residence around the turn of the century. Flattering sketches of him appeared in special editions of the newspaper and all of his accomplishments were touted so that his hometown could bask in reflected glory. In 1904 he donated thirty-six palm trees to Vacaville, and most are still standing where he planted them, along Ulatis Creek in the downtown Creek-Walk. He sold land to the city at favorable prices for various civic projects, such as a new jail. Many churches purchased land from him, including the Japanese Buddhist Temple in 1911. When Pacific Telephone and Telegraph came to town in 1918, it was Thomas who sold the right of way for the poles. He appeared to show a strong sense of civic duty to the town in which he grew up, and the welfare of the community was undoubtedly important to him for both personal and business reasons.

Thomas was in San Francisco April 18, 1906, when the great earthquake and fire struck the city. His offices in the Chronicle Building burned, destroying his entire law library. The Hotel Pleasanton, his city home, also was lost to the flames. Thomas hurried to the Bohemian Club to help protect the club's building and collections of art and books. He had joined this private men's club eight years earlier and was serving on the board of directors at this time. On

View of San Francisco business district after the 1906 Earthquake and Fire. Thomas kept a law office in the old Chronicle Building at the corner of Market and Kearney Streets; its burned-out shell is identified by an arrow. San Francisco Public Library.

the first day of the fire, club members were nervous about the advancing flames, but decided not to empty the building of the club's treasures. They thought the fire would not cross Market Street to reach their location at Post and Grant streets. By the next day, that assumption was proven wrong; only a few paintings were hurriedly saved before the clubhouse was abandoned to its fate. Thomas unwittingly provided his fellow Bohemians with a moment of levity during those last chaotic minutes. A club historian tells the story:

> *Among the horrifying incidents of that fateful evening there was one which brought a thrill of humor to many hearts that so far had felt nothing but sorrow. It was discovered that during the most exciting moments of the work of salvage, [Charley] Dickman had rescued from the office the cards that recorded debts for supplies. On being chided for having been so thoughtless as to preserve evidences of debts that otherwise might never have*

to be discharged, Charley replied, "That was Director Tom Wilson's fault, not mine. How can you fancy any sane excitement that could possibly lead me into perpetuating last month's posted list?[2]

Director Tom redeemed himself by assisting in the Club's financial recovery from the disaster, but he still undoubtedly had to bear up under considerable teasing and banter. The Bohemians loved a good laugh. The Club was known for its tradition of "jinks," both low and high, and its theatrical productions and private entertainments were eagerly anticipated occasions for fun. Thomas participated fully in these jovial traditions and remained active in club affairs after retiring from the Board in 1908. Around this time, he took up residence in Room 19 at the newly-erected clubhouse on Taylor Street. Willis Jepson painted a brief (and slightly disapproving) portrait of Thomas then: "Many years ago, after he had become a mature man, I used to see him contentedly loafing in carefree indolence in the great easy chairs of the Bohemian Club." Thomas was also a member of the Pacific Union Club, another prestigious men's club that, like the Bohemian, is still in existence.

Thomas was a self-described capitalist throughout his later years in San Francisco. He accumulated an extensive portfolio of stocks and bonds; his investments included banks, utilities and water companies, railroads, and highway and school bonds. In addition to managing the Wilson family estate in Vacaville and Solano County, he bought and sold land on his own. At the time of his death in 1921, his estate was valued at $466,631, an impressive fortune for a man whose family came to California in rags.[3]

Health problems overwhelmed him in his final year. Urological complaints that had plagued him for years worsened. By November and December, he was seeing his doctor almost daily and was hospitalized several times to undergo numerous invasive treatments. Ten days before Christmas at age seventy-six, he was hospitalized for surgery, but was released for the holiday. The day after Christmas, he went to his room at the Bohemian Club and shot himself with a .38-caliber revolver. Correnah and her husband, Edward, stopped at the club around 4 p.m. to take Thomas out with them; he was found by a club servant who was sent to fetch him. No one who saw him at the club that day had any inkling of his intentions, but apparently he was convinced that his medical problems were insoluble and he chose to end his suffering.

His will appointed Correnah as executrix. She received half of his estate and the other half was shared equally by his two grand nephews and two grand nieces, four children who were in his words, "all equally dear to me." They were living in Texas, and were direct descendants of Jay, Thomas' brother.

NOTES

1. *Vacaville Reporter,* October 20, 1883, 4.
2. Clay M. Greene, *The Annals of the Bohemian Club: From the Year 1895 to 1906 Inclusive,* 234–236.
3. Probate File No. 33145, San Francisco Court House.

*Jay Crittenden Wilson at approximately twenty years of age. This carte de visite, printed
on heavy card stock, was used as a calling card or formal memento of a visit. On the
reverse is written, "His mother ran the hotel." Harbison Collection, Vacaville Museum.*

ORN IN MISSOURI JUNE 20, 1848, JAY CRITTENDEN WILSON, Luzena's second son, was ten months old when the family began its overland journey west. Luzena does not discuss the daily problems of traveling with young children in a covered wagon, but coping with an infant on the overland trip surely was a challenge. Were the children bored by riding in the wagon all day? Were they ever ill? Luzena provided no details.

Like Thomas, Jay was well-received by the miners and gamblers of early California. Luzena mentions his innocent theft of her bag of gold coins, which he used to build houses in the dusty street outside her El Dorado Hotel in Nevada City. And it was Jay she rescued from his playmates, lest he be hanged as a "squatter" in the Vaca Valley. His carefree days of play were gradually tempered by work and school. His early schooling was probably identical to his older brother's, starting in the village school, then advancing to the Ulatis Academy under Professor Anderson.

At age thirteen, he enrolled in the Collegiate Department at Pacific Methodist College, which had just opened its doors in Vacaville. Although he was the age of a modern high school student, Jay's 1861 curriculum sounds decidedly collegiate by today's standards. In his senior year, for example, he took such courses as Astronomy, International Law, Botany, Geology, Natural Theology, Criticism, and Moral Philosophy.

He was among the dozen seniors who prepared final orations and essays to present at the graduation ceremonies. Jay's speech was titled "The Tyranny of Custom." The ceremony was scheduled for May 18, 1865, but the college building burned to the ground a few days earlier. The college festivities were moved to the lawn of the Young Ladies boarding house on East Main Street, next to the charred ruins. The event celebrated the accomplishments of the young people.

Dr. Lucky, the school president, boasted that the work of the unknown arsonist did not interrupt the school schedule.

Upon completing school, Jay apparently stayed in the Solano County area at first. When registering to vote there, he listed his occupation as railroad agent, age twenty-one. Railroad fever was high in Vacaville and all over the West. Jay's father was the first president of the Vaca Valley and Clear Lake Railroad, and Jay may have worked for this rail line. He did not linger in the area, however, but traveled to San Diego County where he and a partner went into the live-stock business, herding sheep. He wrote to college classmate Melissa Allison in 1870, and two letters provide a glimpse of this twenty-two-year-old man:

April 29, 1870
In the Mountains, San Diego County, California
To: Miss E. Melissa Allison
From: Jay C. Wilson
My ever to be remembered friend:

It may seem late to you for me to undertake to renew a correspondence with one who has ever been to me a friend, both faithful and true, and perhaps I may incur your displeasure by so doing. Notwithstanding I did not ask your permission to renew it. I will attempt to do so hoping that you will at least pardon this one intrusion. As far as the mere idea of receiving letters from Vacaville is concerned, I must say that I take little interest in that. There are some residing in that vicinity whose friendship I prize and whose kind words I will always remember. It is to be presumed that my business in this section is known to any one who took sufficient interest to inquire.

My own opinions have never been my guide for there have always been some gray heads willing to advise. Having been taught now by experience that my own judgment is as good as any one's, I will endeavor here after to allow myself not to hearken to the wisdoms of fifty years ago.

You are able to judge of the beauties of this section at present if you will recall to mind the appearance of Solano on August of 1864. It is just as green and the prospects are just as flattering.

Excitements cannot be of any service in reviving this country now that it has finally collapsed. Some of our worthy friends who have invested their last cent may come out minus at least if they invested during the height of excitement.

I have heard that Charles was in San Diego while I was on the tramp. He is certainly able to understand the situation of things. I have seen your Uncle Robert several times. He is in high good humor, but I fear it is put on for the occasion. Should I not succeed in making ends meet this year, it is only a few leagues to the Apache country and I find on careful examination that I am only half civilized. A total indifference in regard to the result of such matters might seem to presage a certain ruin, but I am not able to find any reason why I should not as well now as ten years hence go to utter ruin. It is said that there is an elixir to all the ills that human flesh is heir to, but as it is not to be found without some more search that I am willing to give, I have long since given up the vain hope of ever finding it.

The Rail Road fever has long since subsided and reason resurged its way where fevered frenzy was want to take the lead. Town lots are not so high but what I, poor as I am, might not succeed in purchasing should I feel so disposed.

I have not discovered that this fine climate has improved my health nor yet impaired. Many come to this unchanging climate to seek health, and from some cause find that it is in some respects an advantage. It will perhaps not be long before we make our advent to the regions of gold. Should I conclude to make another attempt at mining, rest assured you will never see me again. There are certain things must be accomplished before I ever set foot in Solano again.

I occasionally hear some news in regard to your neighborhood that is startling in the extreme, and should some things I have heard hinted prove true, farewell to all my long cherished hopes.

Should this offering of friendship prove unacceptable, I must wish you a long adieu. My address is at present: San Luis Rey, San Diego County, Cal., care of Patrick O'Neil.

Will I have the honor of hearing from you or is this a last adieu from your Obedient Servant.

Jay C. Wilson[1]

FOURTH ANNIVERSARY.
OF
PACIFIC METHODIST COLLEGE,
VACAVILLE.

Friday, May 12th.   Primary Examination.
Sunday, 14th.   Baccalaureate Sermon, Rev. E. K. Miller.
Monday, 15th 8 A. M.   Examination of College Classes.
"   " 7½ P. M.   Primary Exhibition.
Tuesday, 16th, 8 A. M. Examination of College Classes.
"   " 10 A. M.   Meeting of Trustees.
"   " 7½ P. M.   Freshman Exhibition.
Wednesday,17th,8 A.M. Examination of College Classes.
"   " 7½ P.M   Sophomore and Junior Exhibition.
Thursday, 18th.   Annual Commencement.
                       8½ A. M. Address to Ulatus Society. Rev. O. P. Fitzgerald.
                       10½ A. M. Addresses of the Graduating Class.

All persons are invited to attend the above exercises.   W. T. Lucky, President.
P. M. College, May 1st, 1865.

Advertisement in the Solano Press, May 10, 1865. Jay's college graduation exercises were conducted just yards away from the ashen remains of the school building. A critical report on the ceremonies appeared in the same newspaper two weeks later, demonstrating that the firestorm of public sentiment ignited by Lincoln's death was still raging. The writer was appalled that patriotism and American culture were absent from the program and found some speeches treasonable. He said, "the Vacaville College is injuring itself by permitting such intensely Southern exercises to be delivered in public." Solano County Archives.

A careful reading of this letter yields a few clues to Jay's personality. His comparison of the "beauties" of the San Diego area to Solano County in August shows a gift for irony: Solano County in the summer is hot, uniformly dry and definitely not green. The reference to making another attempt at mining and the "regions of gold" is interesting; his brother, Thomas, had tried mining at White Pine, Nevada. Jay doesn't say where his own attempt led him. The startling news he mentioned at the end of the letter may refer to Melissa's courtship with Zebulon Donaldson, another of their classmates at Pacific Methodist College. Jay may have been gently hinting to Melissa that he had hopes of winning her heart himself, should she welcome his advances.

June 9, 1870
San Luis Rey
To: Melissa Allison
From: Jay C. Wilson
My dear Melissa:

Your kind letter of May 28th is just at hand. I have recently been out in the neighborhood of the Colorado Desert. Found plenty of grass and 50,000 head of cattle to eat it. I don't think there is any danger of my losing any more sheep this summer, but perhaps will have some bad luck in the winter.

Eliza Melissa Allison's diploma from Pacific Methodist College. Harbison Collection, Vacaville Museum.

There have not been any incidents worthy of notice in which I have been connected since I wrote to you. An Indian that was driving with us when we were moving our sheep shot himself in the head with my gun, killing him instantly.

I have today come out from San Diego. Uncle Robert was out at the Cuyomac, did not see him. I understand he is likely to have some trouble with the miners of the Julian and Coleman districts. Met Mr. Luco. He told me of the trouble. Found out that Tom had gone to San Francisco. Presume you have seen him or at least heard of him. Yours was the first letter I had received for two months. Presume my mother has written to me frequently. What becomes of the letters I cannot imagine.

The country is vulgarly speaking "caved in" and "given up." The entire region for forty miles from the line of Lower California up to San Luis Obispo is as bare as can be. Think I will leave this country as soon as possible and try the neighborhood of Owens River or Nevada. Every quarter section in the country not on a grant that is not worthless nor destitute of water has been taken up by some one. The Indians occupy some portions and a man in their neighborhood is at their mercy. Anywhere else at the mercy of Mexicans. I still continue to make improvement in Spanish. Can now speak quite well on ordinary topics, but a conversation is still too much for me.

Mr. Cooper is a Spanish scholar. You can learn it if you see fit. You will not find much trouble in learning to telegraph. I'm not sorry on account of the removal of P. M. C. and have no tears of regret to shed if its ultimate fate is as you suppose it will be. Have not felt myself interested in it since Mr. Lucky left.

Am surprised to learn Mamie has gone; presume she will return to Cal. My partner is trying to retire from the sheep business. Hope he will succeed. Will know next time what kind of a man I go in partnership with. He is anxious to get back to Vacaville. Why I cannot say. There is nothing here to attract anyone and I should never advise anyone to come to this county upon any cause. This has always been my opinion. Before I came here I allowed myself to be influenced, but I find my judgment generally proves as good as anyone's. And it shall be my endeavor hereafter to be guided by my opinion in matters and things generally. When I next move, it will be to some place selected altogether by myself.

Have not yet fallen in love with any of the rich Spanish Senoritas and think I know girls in Solano I would prefer in poverty to anyone I have seen in San Diego with wealth. Find on examination that I am not so much disposed to turn rough as I thought at one time I was. However, it will be necessary for me to live more than two or three years and I can then become again civilized.

Expected to hear of Josie's wedding before now. I am glad she is not married and regret very much she cannot know some things that I do. Marriage is an important event in one's life and is generally a turning point. Notwithstanding all the foolishness I talked too young. I have one selected that I will get if I can sometime, for I think she will just suit me. Philip Morse (the professor's brother) has lately married a young lady of San Diego. Met Cyrus Arnold in town. You remember him I presume. He is married the second time. Before I should make such a step, I think I would consider well.

People here are all Democrats. A great many have just come in from Texas. Lots of fellows here that were in the rebel army. I know one man named C. J. Cruts who has lived here since '17 that was a graduate of West Point in the same class with General Grant. All the old settlers here are married to squaws or Spanish women.

Will not weary your patience longer this time. Write me a long letter.
Yours most affectionately, J. C. Wilson

This time, Jay was full of news about several of their mutual friends. He evidently knew that his brother Tom, now divorced, had gone back to San Francisco and that Pacific Methodist College (the P. M. C. he refers to) had moved to another town. After commenting on such general topics, he returned to his thoughts on love and marriage. If Melissa were indeed the young lady he had in mind for himself, Jay was to be disappointed. She married Zebulon Donaldson one year later.

Jay's life took another unexpected turn. He did not choose his next home entirely on his own as he had planned, but went to Texas in early 1873 to find his father and live with him. Mason had settled in McLennan County, south of Waco, and Jay took up residence near the small town of Perry. The two men bought land and Jay began farming. In the early 1880s the railroad came through this part of central Texas, narrowly bypassing Perry. A new town called Moody sprang up alongside the tracks about a mile away, and immediately absorbed all Perry's populace, including the two Wilson men.

The most prominent family in Moody was the Naler clan, headed by William Naler and his wife Martha. Naler had served in the

Melissa Allison's marriage to Zebulon Donaldson was not happy, and she eventually left him to return home. At age 28, she contracted pneumonia and died at the family ranch, leaving her young daughter Julia to the Allison family's care. Hester Allison always believed that her sister died of a broken heart. Harbison Collection, Vacaville Museum.

Confederate Army in the 39th Georgia Infantry. When the Civil War ended, he and his family lived in Georgia before moving to Texas in 1870. Jay, who came from a family of Union sympathizers, didn't allow politics to stand in the way of matrimony; he married Naler's daughter Margaret Jane on the last day of December 1878. The young couple settled into married life in this agricultural community, where Jay raised sheep and cotton. A son, Asa Cohen Wilson, arrived in 1880 and was joined by a daughter, Rowena, four years later. Mason lived in his son's household until his death in 1882, and Jay seemed to be the sole support for his father during those years.

Few other details are known of the family's life in Texas. Presumably they were a fairly typical farm family, working hard and raising children. Recorded deeds show that Jay continued to buy land in the county until at least the turn of the century. Margaret and Jay moved to Dallas around 1905, and lived with Rowena and her husband, Stephen G. Davis. Rowena died in 1909, leaving her husband and a young son. Jay had started a real estate business in Dallas but operated it for only two years. He died in Dallas, August 3, 1910, at age sixty-two, and is buried in Naler Cemetery in Moody, alongside his wife and daughter.

In spite of his long absence from California, there are indications of cordiality between Jay and his siblings. Jay returned to California at least once to assist in the settling of Luzena's estate in 1902. Thomas expressed warm affection for Jay's family in his will, and Jay's son, Asa, named his own son after his Uncle Thomas. Moreover, Correnah bequeathed family pictures, silverware and a fur coat to Jay's granddaughter, Pamela Claire. Of all Luzena's descendants, only Jay left children to pass on the Wilson family name and traditions to future generations.

NOTES

1. Allison Family Collection, Vacaville Museum.

Somewhere in this crowd of teachers and students on East Main Street in Vacaville are Jay, Mason Jr. and Correnah Wilson. All three were pupils at Pacific Methodist College, which was housed in the old Ulatis Academy building shown here with its bell tower. The photographer is looking south from present-day Andrews Park, with Ulatis Creek in the foreground. To the left is a boarding house, with laundry on the line in the rear. Robert Power Collection, Vacaville Museum.

The new year of 1855 was an occasion for celebration in the Wilson family. Luzena gave birth to her third son, Mason Wilson Jr., January 12. Of all the Wilson children, he remains the most mysterious, and no photograph of him has been found. He died shortly before his thirty-third birthday, and left few clues to his life and personality.

At age six, he was a student at Pacific Methodist College in its inaugural year of 1861. The College had a Preparatory Department which functioned as an elementary school. Mason Jr. became a freshman in the Collegiate Department after five years, and tackled such subjects as algebra and geometry. By the school year 1868, however, all the Wilson children disappeared from the rolls. If Mason Jr. pursued an education past the age of 13, no record of it has yet been found. Willis Jepson wrote in his 1939 letter that Mason Jr. had joined his father in Texas during the 1870s, but this does not seem likely. Jepson probably was confusing young Mason with his older brother Jay who moved to Texas.

By age 20, young Mason was working in San Francisco as a clerk for the Montgomery Street brokerage firm of J. M. Walker and Company. Mason Street in San Francisco was his home address. He later took a job as assistant bookkeeper for stockbroker Charles W. Fox, whose offices were on California Street. By this time he was living on Howard Street where Luzena, Correnah and Thomas moved in with him after the 1877 fires consumed the Vacaville family home.

A young music teacher named Caroline Kisling lived nearby with her mother, stepfather, brother, and stepsister. Caroline was three years younger than Mason Jr., and was also a native Californian, born in the Redwood City area. Her father died in the mid-1860s, and her mother, Maria, married San Francisco carriage builder, John Hayes. Caroline and Mason Jr. met in San Francisco, where they were married around 1881.

Mason moved to Lakeport in Lake County near this time, and set up a grocery business. The local newspaper described him as "one of our enterprising young merchants."[1] He was quickly involved in community affairs and was elected secretary of the local Masonic Lodge in December 1880. Luzena visited her son in his new establishment, and perhaps also visited her sister, Emily Hunt Dodson, who lived nearby in Kelseyville with her husband, Dr. W. B. H. Dodson, and family.

Caroline also played a role in Lakeport community life, as evidenced by a May 1882 newspaper report on a church fund-raising event:

> *The strawberry and ice cream festival given by the ladies of the Presbyterian Church on the 19th was a gratifying success. The tables were decorated with flowers in great profusion and excellent taste. The Court room was full and enthusiasm unabated, when at quarter to nine a short literary and musical programme was announced. Selections upon the piano forte were well rendered by Miss Anna Bigerstaff and Mrs. Mason Wilson, who were heartily applauded. Readings were also given by Miss Martha McNair and Messrs. J. L. Woods and S. H. Rice. The strawberries and ice cream rapidly disappeared, but the supply was bountiful. Aside from the purpose, the festival was a very pleasant social episode. The receipts were $86; net proceeds, $57.65.[2]*

At the time of this piano performance, Caroline Wilson was expecting her first child. Her mother and stepsister Josephine visited her that spring, helping in the last months of her pregnancy. Mason Kisling Wilson arrived in late July, welcomed by his proud parents. He was Luzena's second grandson.

Shortly thereafter, Mason Jr. moved his family back to San Francisco to a residence on Eleventh Street. He paid a visit to his hometown of Vacaville in 1883, and told the newspaper he was "much surprised at what he sees and hears of the rapid increase of wealth and population."[3] His visits in later years were also duly noted in the Vacaville Reporter, but by 1886, the news took on a more ominous tone.

> December 11, 1886: *Mason Wilson's condition has improved greatly. He will, we trust, be shortly convalescent.*
>
> January 15, 1887: *Mason Wilson's condition is daily improving and he is expected before long to be occupying his new house.*
>
> January 22, 1887: *Mason Wilson, who for the past two months has been quite ill in SF, arrived home on Tuesday. Although he has thoroughly recovered from his severe illness, his appearance clearly indicates the fierce struggle he has had with the grim monster, but our bracing atmosphere will soon bring back the ruddy hue to his now pallid countenance.*

The healing powers of the Solano County climate were not enough for Mason; he died in San Francisco December 7, 1887, and was buried in the Masonic Cemetery. The obituary in the *Alta California* gave no details, except that the funeral was at his home on Oak Street in San Francisco.

Caroline was left a widow at age 27 with a 5-year-old son. Eventually her mother, Maria, moved in with her, as did her brother and stepsister. She listed herself in the San Francisco Blue Book, a mark of her pride in her social status. By the turn of the century, the family was living together on Eleventh Street in the city; her brother William was a railroad conductor, while Caroline kept house. Mason Kisling Wilson was still in school then, but listed himself in the 1901 city directory as a "collector." The family was probably residing there in April 1906, when the earthquake and fire leveled their entire neighborhood.

Mason Kisling Wilson evidently relocated to San Mateo County after the disaster, where his story ended in sadness. On August 24, 1908, he died in Menlo Park, having been under constant medical care for the last month of his life. The cause of death was pulmonary tuberculosis, but the doctor also noted that cirrhosis of the liver was a contributing factor to his demise. He was employed as a clerk and listed as married, although no information on his wife has been found. He was only 26 years old.

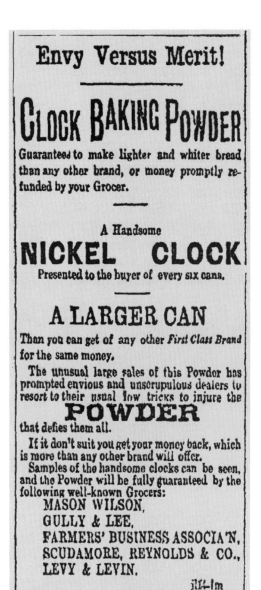

Advertisement for Clock Baking Powder in the Lakeport Bee Democrat, *1882, listed Mason Wilson as one of the merchants who sold the product. Lake County Library.*

Number.	NAME.	Age.	COUNTRY OF NATIVITY.	OCCUPATION.	LOCAL RESIDENCE.
3915	Wilson, William Dunlap	27	Michigan	Farmer	Silveyville
3916	Walker, John	21	Iowa	Farmer	Silveyville
3917	Warren, William Frederick	45	Iowa	Minister	Silveyville
3918	Wiseman, Thomas	46	Missouri	Farmer	Vacaville
3986	Williamson, James	38	Ohio	Musician	Vallejo
4021	Whitaker, Peter	42	Michigan	Engineer	Rio Vista
4033	Watson, William Henry	51	Indiana	Farmer	Elmira
4034	Watson, Samuel Robert	41	Missouri	Farmer	Elmira
4063	Winton, John Wilton	48	Mass.	Machinist	Vallejo
4064	Walsh, Carlisle	26	Cal^{a}	Teamster	Vallejo
4179	Wilson, John Andrew	20	Cal^{a}	Laborer	Vallejo
4124	Webster, Franklin Henry	38	Cal^{a}	Farmer	Benicia
4125	Williams, Albert	52	Sweden	Captain	Green Valley
4152	Wilson, Mason	31	Cal^{a}	Farmer	Vacaville
4154	Walker, Michael	55	Switzerland	Farmer	Vacaville
4165	Myer, Charles Fayette	26	Cal^{a}	Fruit grower	Silveyville
4187	Walker, Rudolf	29	Switzerland	Laborer	Elmira
4188	Wilson, Mortimer Fowler	26	Cal^{a}	Carpenter	Elmira
4189	Wilson, Elijah Jackson	27	Missouri	Farmer	Elmira

Mason Wilson Junior registered to vote in Solano County in 1886 (sixth line from bottom), declaring he was a farmer in Vacaville. Perhaps he was working with Thomas on the family estate. Since he also claimed a San Francisco address that year, he may have been dividing his time between town and country, as Thomas did. Solano County Archives.

Caroline Wilson's name disappeared from public records until 1917, when it turned up in the San Francisco city directory and in a news article. The Native Sons of the Golden West were dedicating a historic monument on the site where California Supreme Court Justice David Terry and United States Senator David Broderick dueled in 1859. Terry and Broderick were bitter political rivals whose animosity became personal. Dueling was acceptable at the time, and the two men met to settle their dispute with pistols. Broderick died of his wounds, and Terry's conduct was hotly debated all over town. Though the rules of honor had been followed, many considered Terry a murderer.

Caroline Wilson was a guest speaker at the dedication and told a story that had been passed down through her stepfather's family. According to the news article,

> *Mrs. Mason Wilson [Caroline] . . . said that on the night before the duel Justice Terry had slept at the home of her uncle, Thomas Hayes, Hayes Street and Van Ness Avenue, and after the duel, Justice Terry had gone to her father's home, Thirteenth and Folsom Streets, and had there thrown himself on an old haircloth couch and moaned his sorrow for having wounded Senator Broderick.*[4]

Thomas Hayes, brother of Caroline's stepfather, was one of Terry's seconds in the duel, and had served as County Clerk in the city. Hayes Valley in San Francisco was named for this family.

After this public appearance, Caroline faded into history. She was last listed in the city directory in 1924. No death record has been located.

NOTES

1. *Lakeport Bee Democrat,* November 26, 1880.
2. *Lakeport Bee Democrat,* May 28, 1882.
3. *Vacaville Reporter,* March 17, 1883, 4.
4. *San Francisco Examiner,* February 23, 1917, 8.

Top: *Lulu Dobbins pasted this photo of her cousin, Correnah, in a scrapbook. Donald Dobbins Collection, Vacaville Museum.*

Above: *Tintype of Correnah as a teenager.*

Right: *Correnah around age eighteen. Both teenage photographs from Carol Buck Collection; Vacaville Museum.*

L UZENA'S LAST CHILD, CORRENAH MOREHEAD WILSON, was born Friday, April 24, 1857. She arrived when the Wilson family was entering a period of prosperity and relative ease; their land titles were secure and they were rapidly becoming one of the richest families in Solano County. Luzena had the money to secure for her only daughter every possible advantage, particularly in education. Correnah fully justified the investment her parents made in her. Trained in the best women's schools of the day, she eventually achieved an academic and social position that Luzena could scarcely have imagined as a pioneer.

Correnah first attended Pacific Methodist College with Jay and Mason Jr. where she was enrolled in the Preparatory Class at the age of four. During six school years she worked her way through the primary grades, but her name does not appear in the class listings after 1867.

At the tender age of twelve, she went off to the College of Notre Dame, a residence school for girls operated by the Catholic Church in San Jose. Today, Notre Dame is an accredited university, but in 1869 it functioned more as a finishing school for girls who would typically stay a year or two. Correnah made the honor roll for general excellence and achieved "premium" awards for piano and drawing during her first year. Grammar, arithmetic, orthography, penmanship and domestic economy were her best subjects. In the realm of character development, she was praised for her overall discipline and application. At the graduation ceremony that ended her first year, she was featured in a drama, the *Witch of Rosenberg*. She was also one of twelve pianists playing as a group on four pianos, whose performance opened the festivities. In her second year, she was named a Distinguished Scholar and received special awards for bookkeeping and domestic economy. Correnah continued to take extra instruction in both music and drawing. According to College ledger books, tuition, board and fees for Correnah cost the Wilsons $498.50 in the school year 1870 to 1871.

Mills Seminary (now Mills College) in Oakland was Correnah's next destination. Mills was founded in Benicia in 1852, and the school moved to Oakland in 1871. Correnah, at age fifteen, became a member of its Junior Middle Class one year later. The curriculum was much more challenging than at Notre Dame. Correnah tackled algebra, natural history, mythology and natural philosophy in her first term, then moved on to geometry, botany, and meteorology for the second half of the year. Languages and arts were electives, available for an extra fee. Correnah always took drawing and painting classes, showing a love of art that remained a lifelong passion. Her senior year classes included literature with an emphasis on Milton, theology and philosophy. When she graduated in 1875, Correnah could easily be regarded as one of California's best educated women. Tuition at Mills was $175 for each twenty-week term, drawing lessons were $20 extra, and oil painting was $40 more. Thus it cost roughly $1,400 to support Correnah through her three years at Mills. Luzena handled these costs on her own, since Mason had abandoned the family four months after Correnah had enrolled. This is yet another measure of Luzena's determination to provide the best for her daughter. Correnah cherished her degree from Mills and remained a loyal alumna her entire life.

Correnah came home to live again in Vacaville at age eighteen. Her life may have seemed somewhat quiet after years away at school, but she and Luzena began to travel together. In fact, they were at Yosemite when the family home burned in June 1877. Shortly after, Correnah moved to San Francisco which would become her permanent home. There she suffered a serious illness in 1881, never specifically identified. During her convalescence Correnah listened to her mother's stories of the early days and wrote them down as faithfully as she could. Correnah was also there the next year to support her mother when Luzena learned that she was a widow.

After a suitable time had passed, the two ladies embarked on a grand tour of Europe. The *Vacaville Reporter* announced that they would set sail May 2, 1883, for an extended tour. Luzena took the railroad back east this time, riding comfortably in a palace car rather than walking beside an ox-drawn wagon. The local paper reported that the trip from New York to London took approximately one month. Their adventures intrigued hometown friends who, by Christmastime, were speculating that Correnah had made a "conquest" while abroad. But they were disappointed.

The rumor which was gaining currency through the public prints that Miss C. M. Wilson, a young lady reared in Vacaville, now traveling in Europe was soon to be married to a Hungarian nobleman is all a hoax. Thus falls flat a romantic story. Miss

Top: *Mills College in the 1870s.*
Alumnae Association of Mills College.
Right: *Art Class at Mills College.*
Special Collections, F. W. Olin
Library, Mills College.

Wilson and her mother will return in March to San Francisco, having been absent
one year on their tour.[1]

Correnah married two years later. Her September 8, 1886 wedding to an
American gentleman was described in a San Francisco newspaper:

> *The wedding of Miss Correnah Wilson and Mr. E. C. Wright was very quietly cel-*
> *ebrated on Wednesday last at the First Unitarian Church, by the pastor, Rev. Horatio*
> *Stebbins. The ceremony was witnessed by a small party of relatives and friends, and*
> *immediately after the nuptials the happy couple started on their bridal tour. The wed-*
> *ding guests included Mr. and Mrs. Fred Crocker, Mrs. Lansing, the Misses McGerry,*

*Mr. and Mrs. A. Wigmore, and the bride's moth-
er and brothers.*[2]

Edward Clark Wright was the assistant general
auditor of the Southern Pacific Railroad at the
time, with offices in San Francisco. He had
arrived in California in 1870 to work as a clerk for
the Central Pacific Railroad, obtaining the job
through family connections. He was a first cousin
of Charles Crocker, one of the "Big Four" who
built the railroad that linked the West to the East.[3]
Edward worked his way up the corporate ladder,
rising from clerk to chief clerk auditor. When the
Central Pacific consolidated with Southern Pacific Railroad in 1884, he became assistant general
auditor, then general auditor, and finally, secretary
and assistant controller.

*A formal portrait of Mrs. Edward
C. Wright was published in a book
written to honor the Woman's Board
of the Panama Pacific Exposition, of
which she was a director. California
State Library.*

Though Edward's career in California appeared
to be a steady climb to success, he had encountered true hardship early in life. He was the third
of seven children born to Dr. Julius Wright and
his wife Elizabeth in 1844 on Long Island, New
York. Edward could count among his distinguished Wright ancestors a New
England great-grandfather who helped build Dartmouth College, as well as a
grandfather and five uncles who were physicians. His father's sister, Elizabeth
Wright, was the mother of Charles Crocker. With such a promising background,
Edward may have had expectations of a professional career in the Northeast; at
age eighteen, though, he was working as a clerk. Then came the Civil War.

Edward volunteered in the Twenty-first New Jersey Infantry, in order to serve
alongside a friend who was at Princeton College. He signed up September 8,
1862, and his company left immediately for the front; ten days later he was on the
battlefield at Antietam, Maryland. He was wounded by a gunshot as he and his
fellow soldiers charged Salem Heights near Fredericksburg, May 3, 1863. Army
surgeons amputated his leg midway between the knee and the ankle, probably
on the battlefield, and he was taken to a hospital in Washington, D.C. His dis-
charge came June 13, just as his tour of duty came to an end. Edward, who had
earlier been promoted to corporal, was classified as a wounded veteran and
awarded a pension of $8 per month.

According to his medical release papers, nineteen-year-old Edward was a blue-eyed, sandy- haired man of medium height, about five feet nine inches tall. His oldest brother George came to Washington, D.C. to escort him home to New-town, Long Island. Since Edward had a "good stump," according to the Army doctors, he was fitted with an artificial leg by a New York City physician. Edward did not stay long in the East, and within three years, he was living in Leaven-worth, Kansas. His activities and occupation in Kansas are unknown, but while there, he applied for an increase in his pension. A few years later, he came West to work for the Central Pacific Railroad.

After Correnah and Edward's marriage, the newlyweds settled into life in San Francisco. They usually lived in residence hotels and did not buy a home of their own for decades. Edward, it seemed, led a quiet life; his name does not often appear in the newspapers. Correnah, however, immediately involved herself in the social and cultural life of San Francisco. She was thirteen years younger than her husband and she devoted her considerable energies to her role as a society matron and club woman. Though he may not have craved the spotlight himself, Edward accompanied his wife to various social functions.

Correnah was invited to join the Century Club of California in 1889, organized that year by prominent women, such as Mrs. Phoebe Hearst, mother of the famed William Randolph Hearst. The club's programs and projects centered on educational topics, including music, fine arts, drama, literature, current events and science. Social events were also important to the membership. Correnah pre-sented a speech titled, "A Woman's Reminiscences of Early Days," at a club meeting in 1893, reading Luzena's chapter describing Sacramento in 1851, and the family's arrival in Vaca Valley. Through the years she participated in a for-mal debate regarding government ownership of railroads, discussed Japanese art, and chaired the club's Spring Art Exhibition. In this last project, she bravely determined to reject any member's paintings that were deemed inferior. Her own pastels were occasionally displayed, but it is not clear who passed judgment upon their quality![4]

Correnah was elected president of the club for the year 1904–1905, and her major duty was supervising the construction of a new clubhouse at the corner of Sutter and Franklin Streets. She waged battle with the Board of Public Works over alleged ordinance violations, oversaw the financing of the venture through private bond sales, served as liaison to the building contractors and coordinated the work of numerous club committees. In a good-natured tone, she said in her annual report, "In all, 97 meetings have been held, and at 96 of them I have presided. Have I not earned a rest?"[5] She proved to be a gifted administrator and developed her executive skills on the job. Her own words summarized the experience:

> *Upon the day I took the chair I promised you that I would do my best, and I have kept my word. It has been a strenuous year. Almost every day has brought its problem, and at times I have been required, by virtue of my office, to make immediate decisions upon important matters upon which I would have been glad to take better judgement than my own. I have watched the building of the Club-house with the same care and attention that I would give to my own home. . . . I have inspected the work almost daily, and I have a personal acquaintance with almost every nail in the structure. If you are pleased, I am rewarded. I have enjoyed the work of the Club, and the work of building, and most of all I have enjoyed your cordial greetings week by week.*

She retired from office content with her contributions, and the gala reception which marked the grand opening in October 1905 was dedicated to her. The San Francisco Earthquake in April 1906, inflicted only minor damage to the club's chimney. The ensuing fire that consumed much of the city was stopped before it reached Franklin Street, sparing the newly-finished structure. When the club undertook remodeling in 1914, Correnah was pressed into service to chair that committee; this time she worked on the project with noted architect, Julia Morgan, a fellow club member and the designer of Hearst Castle in San Simeon. The Century Club building still stands today and the club remains an active part of the cultural and intellectual life of San Francisco. Four of Correnah's paintings are part of the club's art collection, another tangible reminder of her legacy.

After the 1906 Earthquake, Correnah and Edward lived abroad, as did many other prosperous San Franciscans. Edward had retired from Southern Pacific six years earlier, and had taken a position as treasurer with Pacific Improvement Company, a real estate development firm that had created such planned communities as Hope Ranch on the oceanfront in Santa Barbara. He retired completely from active business in 1906, and consequently, they were free to travel. Around 1910, they returned from Europe and made their home in the Hotel Bellevue.

San Francisco took great pride in its recovery from disaster and wanted an opportunity to announce its renaissance to the world. The opening of the Panama Canal in 1914 provided the inspiration, and the Panama-Pacific Exposition of 1915 was the spectacular result. The Exposition had all the elements of a world's fair and all the attractions of an amusement park. The Palace of Fine Arts is the only Exposition building left standing today, but at least a dozen more temporary palaces were erected on the 635-acre site along the waterfront.

Correnah and many other socially prominent women threw themselves into the effort to bring this great event to the world. Committees were formed under the leadership of Mrs. Hearst, and numerous tasks assigned. Once again, Correnah worked alongside the upper echelon of San Francisco society. The job of the Woman's Board was to "furnish, maintain and administer" the California Host Building. Correnah worked with the designers to ensure the building would accommodate the handsome art and furniture destined for its rooms.[6] She also honored Luzena's memory by assisting in the erection of a monument to pioneer mothers. The women handled many other jobs, including official hostess responsibilities, traveler's aid and publicity. They were self-financed, and raised all the money for their projects through the private sale of shares.

Correnah's energy for worthy projects seemed boundless at this point in her life. Her abiding affection for Mills College led her to accept a position on its board of trustees in 1914. She was promptly selected as a member of a search committee to identify potential candidates for the presidency of the college. She

Correnah and Edward Wright purchased this gabled house in the Cow Hollow neighborhood of San Francisco. Perched on one of the city's many hills, the home offered expansive views of the Bay. Tom and Anne Morton.

and two other women conducted a two-year search, which culminated in the appointment of Dr. Aurelia Reinhardt, a native San Franciscan, as Mills' president in 1916. For twenty-seven years the college flourished under Dr. Reinhardt's leadership. She was a tireless recruiter and fund raiser, who guided the college skillfully through the Great Depression, as well as two world wars. To enhance Mills' academic reputation, Dr. Reinhardt worked to revise the curriculum and provide an excellent teaching faculty. A dynamic public speaker with a dramatic personal presence, she brought the college out of obscurity and into respect.[7]

Correnah's first term on the Mills board lasted four years. Then in 1918, the Mills Alumnae Association elected her to represent them for three more years as the first alumnae trustee. Correnah stayed active in the alumnae organization and the Mills Club all her adult life, serving a term as president of the latter.

The relationship between Correnah and Dr. Reinhardt began rather formally, and their early correspondence often dealt with the college funding problems. After Correnah retired as trustee, a cordial friendship developed between the two women; their letters reflect a growing intimacy that would become increasingly comforting to Correnah in her later years. Formal Victorian manners still prevailed in their day; the two women knew one another for ten years before they began addressing each other by their first names.

During the 1920s, Correnah remained active in social and cultural circles in the city. She was an early supporter of the San Francisco Opera, and one of the original box holders for the 1923 season. All her companions in Box No. 20 were women; it seems that Edward was not the only husband who declined to attend. She went often, sometimes as a guest in the box of Judge G. E. Crocker and Mrs. William Mills. Her correspondence with Dr. Reinhardt detailed a theater trip to New York, where she bemoaned the fact that she was too late for the musical season. Art continued as a central passion. She sat for a formal portrait by Girard Hale, posing in front of a black and gold Japanese screen; the society pages of the newspapers featured the painting's unveiling. Edward and Correnah regularly traveled by car up and down the West Coast. One of her pastels of the Monterey Coast, now in a private collection, is evidence that she still pursued her own art. In 1922, she became involved in politics by joining the California League of Women Voters.

By 1921, the Wrights had purchased a home of their own, with Thomas' financial help. It was a gracious brown shingle house, three stories tall, a suitable home for a family of their social position. Thomas was then officially residing at the Bohemian Club, but he co-signed for this property, evidently wanting to help Correnah obtain the home she desired. His suicide in December that year deprived her of her last brother, but in his will, Thomas gave her and Edward clear title to the house as a final gift.

The Wrights were abroad again by 1924, on a tour of England with friends. They were having lunch at a restaurant in the little town of Worksop when Edward, who was eighty years old, fell. His left thigh bone was broken and he was hospitalized; he died a week later, with Correnah at his bedside. She brought his body back to San Francisco, and he was buried with military honors in the Presidio Cemetery.

Widowed at age sixty-seven, Correnah maintained her home and social commitments for a decade more. She met friends for luncheons at fashionable places, and often entertained in her home. Like her mother, she enjoyed people and took pleasure in good company. Around 1928, she went to Europe again, this time to Italy where she painted the watercolors she eventually donated to the Century Club. At age seventy-six, she joined the California branch of the National Society of the Colonial Dames of America. To become a member, she had to show that she had a male ancestor living in one of the thirteen original colonies before 1750. She proved her descent from her Stanley forefathers, indicating her pride in her mother's family and her own knowledge of her Stanley genealogy.

Early in 1934, she decided to sell her home and dispose of most of her possessions. It was a lengthy process, described in a letter to Dr. Aurelia Reinhardt:

> *I am packing industriously a little every day, and already the house has a strange empty look, although there is still much in it. I am eating from dishes that look like remnants from the 5 cent and ten cent [store] but the beds still function and the doors are wide open for you whenever you care to come—and my heart will be open even when the house doors close.*[8]

She was planning to sail to Japan in the fall and was eager to set all her affairs in order. The *San Francisco Call* reported that she had an "elaborate reception" in the house as a farewell gesture.[9] After breaking up her household, she moved into the Women's Athletic Club on Sutter Street, where quite a few elderly women took rooms. From there, she wrote to her friend Dr. Reinhardt July 30th:

> *My dear: I was so sorry to miss you yesterday—I had lunch at the Beach and went afterward to the concert—but alas! in company less stimulating than yours. I am busy with the last minute preparations for my departure, but am really in my room a good deal between times and beg that if you are in town you will drop in to see me. . . . I do want to have a chat with you. Affectionately and devotedly, Correnah W. Wright.*[10]

Correnah, age seventy-seven, set sail for the Orient on the ship, *President Coolidge,* in early August. She planned to visit a friend in Japan, then travel on to Manila and Europe. Shortly after her arrival in Yokohama, she died of a heart attack. All three San Francisco newspapers printed obituaries, calling her a "prominent San Francisco club woman" and "society leader," while detailing her good works and accomplishments.[11] Her ashes were returned to San Francisco and scattered there, according to instructions in her will, which was drawn up only three months before her death.

She had no children, and remembered many dear friends with her bequests. These were quite specific: her Steinway piano, jewelry, silverware, household

Photograph of Correnah was probably taken in her own garden in San Francisco. The ease and comfort of her surroundings speak eloquently of how quickly the Wilson family succeeded in California, leaving Luzena's early struggles and hardship behind them. California Historical Society.

effects and paintings were all designated as gifts to various people. The estate was valued at $46,714.00 after expenses, and was left in trust to provide regular income for five people, two of whom were daughters of one of Correnah's cousins. Upon the death of any of those five, that portion of the estate reverted to the Mills College Department of Fine Arts as a memorial to Luzena Stanley Wilson. The last of the five legatees, Correnah Osgood, died in 1980.[12] Shortly thereafter, Mills College created the Correnah Wright Lecture Series on Contemporary Art, which continues to bring prominent artists to the campus every year. The Series is still funded by the endowment from Correnah.

NOTES

1. *Vacaville Reporter,* January 5, 1884, 1.
2. *San Francisco Call,* September 14, 1886, 3.
3. *San Francisco Examiner,* August 21, 1924, 12. This obituary claimed that Edward Wright and Charles Crocker were cousins. The relationship was confirmed by Edward's christening records, Neil Carothers' article on Crocker genealogy, the 1850 and 1860 Census of Queens County, New York, and the Vital Records of Windsor, Massachusetts.
4. Unpublished documents furnished by Mrs. Henry Gibbons, Historian, Century Club of California, San Francisco.
5. Seventeenth Annual Report of the Century Club, 16.
6. Anna Pratt Simpson, *Problems Women Solved,* 97.
7. George Hedley, *Aurelia Henry reinhardt,* 80-81, 91.
8. Letter to Aurelia Reinhardt, May 9, 1934, Special Collections, F. W. Olin Library, Mills College.
9. *San Francisco Call,* April 25, 1964, 8.
10. Letter, July 30, 1934 (Special Collections).
11. *San Francisco Examiner,* September 13, 1934, 19; *San Francisco Chronicle,* September 13, 1934, 28; and *San Francisco Call,* September 12, 1934, 2.
12. Probate File No. 67899, San Francisco Court House.

Dr. William J. and Eliza Hunt Dobbins are pictured in a carriage outside their home, sometime before 1892. The brick front of the house was damaged in an earthquake that year in Vacaville; the Dobbins' daughter Lou and her sister-in-law were trapped inside under the rubble for a short time but emerged with only bruises. Eleanor Nelson Collection, Vacaville Museum.

FIVE OF LUZENA'S SIBLINGS CAME TO CALIFORNIA during the Gold Rush years, while the others remained in the East. A brief sketch of the lives of the other Hunt sons and daughters will complete the portrait of this nineteenth century family.

Quaker records list the births of nine children to Asa and Diana Hunt. Although their son William told his family there were ten, research to date has not located a tenth child. The first four Hunt offspring were girls born in North Carolina. Rebecca, born 1814, died very young. Lydia, born 1817, was disowned by the Quakers at age nineteen for the same infractions that caused Luzena's ouster; no trace of Lydia's later life has yet been found. The third daughter was Luzena, whose life is well-chronicled. Martha D. Hunt, born 1821, married Daniel Mendenhall at the New Garden Meeting House in 1840; they emigrated to Indiana and raised eight children there.[1] It appears Martha remained in unity with the Quaker discipline throughout her life. The five remaining Hunts all became Californians.

Eliza Hunt (1825–1907) initially remained in Missouri where she married Dr. William Jackson Dobbins in February 1850. Having received encouragement from sister Luzena and brother William, Eliza and William Dobbins came west, living in Placerville, the Feather River area and Sacramento before finally settling in the Vaca Valley in 1854. Dr. Dobbins practiced medicine briefly upon his arrival in California but soon turned to more lucrative pursuits such as hotel keeping and livestock. He was both a rancher and a farmer in Vacaville, running sheep herds and cultivating grain and orchard crops on his large ranch. He and Eliza built a two-story brick home at the corner of present-day Dobbins and Cernon Streets. Although damaged by an earthquake in 1892, the house was rebuilt with wood and survived until the 1970s. Like the Wilsons, the Dobbins were a wealthy family and prominent in Vacaville's community affairs. Eliza had her share of sorrow, mainly in regard to her six children. Her first two sons became attorneys, but both preceded her in death, one at age thirty-nine, the other at forty-five. The third child, a daughter, passed away at age two.[2] Her third son Jeff had a fiery temperament which led him to tragedy; he shot and killed a man in a dispute over a card game in 1900. At age forty-one, he was sentenced to life in prison at San Quentin. Dr. Dobbins threw the family fortune into Jeff's legal defense and numerous appeals, but the appeals were lost along with much of the family's wealth.

The last two Dobbins children had successful careers and families. Sterling P. Dobbins became a prominent citizen, businessman, and Vacaville's mayor in 1906. Lulu, the youngest, was the apple of her mother's eye and a favorite of her father's too; in fact, she may have been spoiled. At age thirteen, she wanted to leave her music lesson early; when her teacher refused she denounced him as an "old fool."[3] The teacher promptly reprimanded her, but Dr. Dobbins was incensed at the teacher and retaliated by beating the teacher on the head with a walking stick; the courts fined Dobbins $100. Lulu went on to lead a settled life, marrying her first cousin, Dillon D. Dodson, and they raised their family in Red Bluff, California.

Both Eliza and William Dobbins are buried in the family vault in the old section of the Vacaville Cemetery.

Alvis Hunt, birth date unknown, traveled west with his siblings. On April 18, 1849, he married Melissa Ann Hunt in Andrew County, Missouri, and their bridal tour consisted of a cross-country trek via wagon train to California.[4] In the fall of 1850, they were living in El Dorado County, working as tavern keepers; Alvis was listed as twenty-five years old and Melissa as nineteen. Their real estate was worth $1,500 and they had a servant, Squire Brown, an African–American from Kentucky. Alvis and his brother, William, according to the latter's story, also traded livestock and hauled freight to the mining towns, while their sisters and Melissa operated a hotel–tavern in Hangtown. In 1851, they closed the hotel and the Hunt siblings relocated to Cacheville, near present-day Woodland, to expand the livestock business. Alvis died the next year; Melissa's fate is unknown.

The seventh child was William Gaston Hunt (1827–1899) who became a wealthy and influential pillar of the community of Woodland, California. William arrived in California in September 1849 and was in business with Alvis until death parted them. Soon after establishing himself in Yolo County, William married Jennie Day and then purchased a ranch which would be the founda-

William Gaston Hunt. and his wife, Jennie
Day Hunt. Fairfield Public Library.

tion of his family's fortune. For the first ten years he was a sheep rancher; then he grew wheat and orchard crops. Later he invested in warehouses and started purchasing and distributing grain regionally. After twenty years, he moved his family to Woodland and took a leadership role in developing the city infrastructure, founding a bank and supporting various charities. During this time, he accumulated more wealth in real estate. He maintained an enthusiasm for progress and at age sixty-nine, wrote an article for the local paper headlined, "Come, wake up, many golden opportunities await local capitalists."[5] William and Jennie Hunt had three children: a son Alvis, and two daughters Alice and Rowena. Both daughters attended Mills College and Rowena later named one of her own daughters after Correnah Wilson Wright. Like Luzena, William and Jennie enjoyed travel and included the southern and eastern United States, Europe, Alaska, Hawaii and Mexico in their various journeys. William retired in Oakland, California, where he is buried.

Emily Hunt (1830–1914) was living with her brother William in Cacheville when she visited Sacramento in the fall of 1851. There she met Dr. William Burr Harrison Dodson, whose medical offices were on J Street, just a few blocks from Luzena's old hotel. They were married the next year and settled in Sacramento City. Dr. Dodson soon found that the practice of medicine did not suit him and gave it up. In his lifetime, he pursued various careers, including newspaper editor, farmer, stockman, hotelkeeper, druggist, postmaster and state legislator. Emily accompanied him to Kelseyville in Lake County, and then to Red Bluff. Along the way she bore him ten children, seven of whom survived to adulthood.[6] Emily's four sons chose careers from the long list of their father's endeavors. Like almost all the other Hunt descendants, they appear to have been solid citizens. Emily died at the outbreak of the first world war, and it is remarkable to contemplate the extent to which the world had changed during her eighty-four years. Her obituary hailed her as a "pioneer lady."[7]

The last sister, Harriet, came west with her family, but few traces of her presence have been found. She apparently stayed with Emily while their two brothers moved the family from Placerville to Cacheville. After Emily's marriage, Hatty lived with her sister and brother-in-law in Sacramento where the census taker listed her under her nickname. There the trail grows cold; the youngest of her family, Harriet's fate is unknown.

NOTES

1. Quaker records, Family Search Pedigree File, Family History Center, LDS Church; and 1850 Census, Miami County, Indiana.

2. Pioneer Files and Cemetery Records, Solano County Genealogical Library, Vacaville, California.

3. Limbaugh and Payne, *Vacaville: The Heritage of a California Community*, 94.

4. The Andrew County marriage record spells his name Alvius and hers Melise Ann Hunt, indicating that Hunt was also her maiden name. The 1850 California Census spells their names Melissa and Alva.

5. *Yolo Semi-Weekly Mail,* April 7, 1896.

6. Biographical Information File, California State Library; and 1900 Census, Tehama County, California.

7. *Red Bluff Weekly News,* September 11, 1914, 1.

Notes on the First Edition of
LUZENA STANLEY WILSON: '49er

EUCALYPTUS PRESS was housed in the garage of Rosalind A. Keep's cottage on the Mills College campus in Oakland, California. Miss Keep worked by day for the college in various academic and administrative posts, but in her leisure time she taught herself to print books. All her books were typeset by hand, printed on a massive Washington hand-press, and displayed high standards in materials and craftsmanship. Luzena's memoir is generally regarded as one of the finest of the 110 titles published by Miss Keep between 1932 and 1950.

The illustrator for the 1937 book was Kathryn Uhl who taught life drawing in the art department at Mills. Miss Uhl established an artistic reputation as an illustrator, lithographer and enamelist; her work has been exhibited at the Crocker Art Museum and in numerous other collections. Her husband, Carlton Ball, was a noted ceramicist and head of the Mills Art Department. Enamel murals by Fred Uhl Ball, her son, can be found on many public buildings in Sacramento. One of her precise and detailed drawings introduced each of Luzena's ten chapters in the first edition; they are reproduced here in this new volume.

Both Eucalyptus Press at Mills College and the heirs of Kathryn Uhl Ball have welcomed this new edition; their support is gratefully acknowledged.

ACKNOWLEDGMENTS

RESEARCHING THIS BOOK was more than mere discovery of facts and historical anecdotes. I also found numerous resourceful, intelligent people to help and encourage me. To each of them I am grateful.

Sabine Goerke-Schrode was a valued mentor and professional resource who gave early advice on structure, read every draft and assisted in key research. Karen Nolan's skills as a writer and editor were of great assistance in critiquing my writing style and providing focus. All my readers offered wise counsel and perspective; my thanks go to Jerry Bowen, Georgia Chun, David Allan Comstock, Bert Hughes, Nancy Kawata and Chris Meade.

I also appreciate the help of Robert Armstrong, Yvonne Ashmore, Robert Bates, Ruth Begell, Bob and Eleanor Brouhard, Dr. Michael Carney, Keith and Diane Cary, Heidi Casebolt, Anita Crabtree, Mrs. Henry Gibbons, Terry and Larry Grill, Susan Haas, Louise Henry, Mary Higham, Cora Lee Jones, Pat Keats, Ruth Kuntz, Betty Lampen, Joann Leach Larkey, Pat Leiser, Jo Ann Levy, Clyde Low, Shawn Lum, Jim Moehrke, Nancy Morebeck, Tom and Anne Morton, Frank Pangburn, Theodore Perkins, Norma Rayl Rock, Mrs. Clarke W. Thornton, Nancy Weston, Leonard Vasquez.

It was truly wonderful to meet Pamela Dixon, Luzena's great-great-granddaughter, and her husband Marvin Dixon; their enthusiasm for this project was gratifying.

Many librarians, archivists and researchers answered questions. At Mills College, I am indebted to Janice Braun, Judy Mollica, Kathleen Walkup and Marilyn Mary for their cheerful assistance. Gwen Gosney Erickson of the Friends Historical Collection at Guilford College took time to answer numerous queries. In addition, I received help from Dr. Alvin Anderson, William Buckner, Matt Buff, Sister Marie Egan, SND, Pat Johnson, and Ruth Kuntz. The staff at the California State Library, Solano County Archives, Solano County Genealogical Society, Vacaville Heritage Council and Vacaville Museum were gracious and knowledgeable.

My publisher Carl Mautz believed in this book even before it was written and provided the encouragement and support to make it happen. Rosemarie Mossinger has been a patient editor and gentle instructor as the book took shape, facing each challenge with grace and humor. It was an honor to have Gary Kurutz write the introduction to this new edition.

Finally, thanks to my husband Bill Spurlock who worked extensively on the illustrations and was involved in countless other tasks. As always, he helped me achieve my goal.

FERN L. HENRY

ORIGINAL 1937 INTRODUCTION
BY FRANCIS P. FARQUHAR

MRS. LUZENA STANLEY WILSON'S ACCOUNT of her pioneer years in California is of significance not only for the vividness of the portrayal but for the circumstances that led to the preservation of the story. In 1881 her only daughter, Correnah, was convalescing from a serious illness. To make the time pass less slowly, Mrs. Wilson recounted her early experiences and the daughter wrote them down in long hand. Years later they were typewritten and bound, and one of the two copies was given to the Mills College Library. On the last page of the reminiscences there is subscribed: I have written my mother's story as nearly as I could in her words. Correnah Wilson, April, 1881.

Her many friends will recall that Correnah Wilson was graduated from Mills in 1875, that she was the first Alumnae Trustee of the college, and that she left to her alma mater beautiful examples of Oriental art. Always interested in art and literature, she took a leading part in many cultural activities. At one time she was president of the Century Club in San Francisco. In 1886 she married Edward Clark Wright who was for many years connected with the railroad business in California. Mr. Wright died in 1924. Ten years later Mrs. Wright sailed for the Orient where she planned to spend some time in travel, but her death occurred in Yokohama September 11, 1934, shortly after her arrival in Japan.

It is characteristic of Mrs. Wright that she left no memoranda to accompany the manuscript she gave to Mills College. For her the experiences set forth were self-explanatory, like works of art, needing no labels. The narrative gives a vivid picture of the incessant struggle of pioneer life. It brings out especially the qualities of buoyancy and cheerfulness that helped to make conquest possible. Hearing Mrs. Wilson's story, in her own words, we come to know her well, long before she and her family are driven out of Sacramento by the flood. She reveals herself in every word and act. Yet, curiously enough, notwithstanding her ability to paint the scene and to sketch casual characters, we learn from her very little about her husband and her children. Nor is there any intimation of what went before or what came after these few years of emigration and pioneering.

Of what came before, little enquiry is necessary. It was undoubtedly the same story, in general outline, as that of hundreds of other families—restless prairie farming. And the sequel we know to some extent—establishment in moderate economic security with more and more means and leisure for cultivated enjoyment as time went on. There is no need for elaboration upon the themes of these earlier and later periods—the dramatic quality was crowded into the central portion.

One is concerned, however, with a few facts; especially as the narrative touches the foundations of California history. Although not once does Mrs. Wilson think to mention her husband's name, we have a natural desire to know something of him. It might be expected that, as he was one of the earliest settlers in Vacaville, the histories of Solano County would give an account of him. Very little is recorded of that town, however, until the period of railroads and agricultural statistics and we have to use a good deal of conjecture in piecing together the fragments of earlier history. An early plat of the townsite shows a considerable area as owned by Mason Wilson, and in one of the "blocks" is shown the Wilson house. It is at about the site of the brick building which now stands on the corner of Davis Street and Main Street, just where the latter turns across the bridge over Ulattis Creek. This land was formerly part of a grant to Manuel Vaca. At precisely what date the Wilsons acquired it, is not known, but it must have been very soon after their arrival. It is not entirely clear from Mrs. Wilson's narrative whether that was in the spring of 1851 or 1852. The fire that destroyed Nevada City was in March 1851, and, although that does not allow full eighteen months for their residence there, it seems to agree with other statements in the story and establish 1851 as the date of their settling at Vacaville.

The records of Solano County show that Mason Wilson, farmer, of Vacaville, was born in Kentucky about 1807. He was, accordingly, forty-two years old when he came to California. His wife, Luzena, was some fourteen years younger. We may picture her, therefore, as about twenty-eight at the time of the journey. The two children who came with them were Thomas, about three, and Jay, less than a year old. Two other children were born in Vacaville—Mason, in 1855, and Correnah, in 1857.

In the *Alta California* of July 17, 1860, a traveler writes of his tour through Solano County. He tells of Vaca's land, now divided among a number of purchasers, one of them a Mr. Wilson. "Mr. Wilson," he says, "bought a tract of about seven hundred acres where the road crosses the valley, and on the bank of the creek built an inn." And not a word of Mrs. Wilson! I am quite sure that Mrs. Wilson would not have protested against this omission—in fact, she would doubtless have deprecated any mention of the part she played in the founding of the town of Vacaville. Fortunately, however, in the narrative preserved by her daughter, we have sufficient testimony to establish the fact that her part was not merely one of "feminine influence." It was that, of course; but it was also just as vigorous and physically productive as that of any miner, farmer, teamster, or builder. After reading these reminiscences, we hasten to correct the statement of the *Alta's* correspondent and declare that whereas, on the bank of the creek at Vacaville, Mr. Wilson built an inn, Mrs. Wilson ran it.

Francis P. Farquhar
San Francisco, California
April, 1937

APPENDIX II

THE JEPSON LETTER

TWO YEARS AFTER THE FIRST PUBLICATION OF LUZENA'S MEMOIR, Dr. Willis L. Jepson (1867–1946) wrote Francis Farquhar to debunk the myths he perceived in Farquhar's introduction to the book. At the time, the two men were residents of Berkeley and active in the Sierra Club. They clearly were acquainted but the full extent of their personal relationship is unknown.

Jepson was the most influential California botanist of his day. His 1925 *Manual of the Flowering Plants of California* rapidly became the standard guide for native plant identification. It remains in use today, constantly updated, and is known familiarly as the *Jepson Manual*. His name and legacy also live on at the Jepson Herbarium, a research facility at the University of California, Berkeley. Valuable though he was as a scientist, he was described by a faculty colleague as a very difficult person. His correspondence, which is voluminous, makes interesting reading as a character study. And the letter about Luzena, printed below in its entirety, is valuable even though many of Jepson's recollections cannot be proven or discredited. While acknowledging Luzena's many virtues, he was also firmly critical of her and her family. The net effect renders Luzena more fully human, even if Jepson overstated her faults.

This letter is printed courtesy of the Jepson Herbarium, University of California, Berkeley.

March 21, 1939
Mr. Francis Farquhar
2900 Garber Street
Berkeley, California
Dear Mr. Farquhar:

"Luzena Stanley Wilson, Forty-niner" has this moment been under my eye. A rigid selection of dramatic and spectacular episodes, it is remarkable, almost incredible, how much is left out. At the time or very shortly after the time that the Wilsons settled at the Ulatis Creek crossing, W. J. Dobbins settled in Vaca Valley and owned the greater portion of the lower valley floor. His wife was sister to Mrs. Wilson and yet Luzena Wilson never mentions her. Luzena Wilson lived in that valley from about 1851 near forty years, until her death, and yet she mentioned by name not a single neighbor of the village or of the near-by ranches. Even more curious still she does not mention the final completed Wilson House which stood at the corner of what is now Main and Davis streets near the present bridge over the Ulatis. It was a two-story brick building, substantial for its day, and everything about it bespoke solidity and the comfort of a first-class country inn. The horse stages from Vallejo stopped in front of the wide door that opened into a large traveler's room with a great fire-place on the east side and a resplendent bar in the southwest corner. From here a door led into a large well-appointed dining room whose windows looked out onto the spaces of a pleasant garden at the rear.

Mrs. Wilson, having grown opulent, gave up personal care of the hotel finally and built herself an attractive residence on the north side of the street where all was open space save for a livery stable and possibly one shop. In that day fire was a great scourge. The village had no water works nor running water, and no fire-company. Three times in early days, say about 1870 to 1884, during the prevalent southwest trades of summer, the central portion of the village was more or less completely erased. Mrs. Wilson's home passed out in one of these fires. She does not mention her fine residence or the fire.

The energy and native capacity of Mrs. Wilson was so great that perhaps it is natural we find her deriding shiftless neighbors. The whole of Vaca Valley and the neighboring valleys were settled mainly by Southerners—families from Virginia, Kentucky and especially Missouri. The Missourians have long been considered fair game for derision and banter. Unquestionably the Yankees are much "smarter," but relatively as many or more Missourians in Vaca Valley held on to their ranches during the panic years of 1873, 1894 and 1932 as did Yankees. The men of the valley who have defrauded their neighbors, however, in the grand Stanford–Huntington manner, have been Yankees all with the exception of one Southerner.

Mrs. Wilson mentions interestingly the beginnings of the Pacific Methodist College in Vacaville. It is a pity she said so little. This college, a tribute to the idealism of the ranchers of Southern origin, was started long before a state university was thought of. The college building was a substantial structure in the classical tradition and its curriculum was along classical lines. I do not find the Wilsons did anything for its endowment. The Wilson land hemmed in closely the original plat of the town on the west, south and east; the Dobbins land on the north. More land for building lots was urgently needed. Many many families came to live in the village on account of the college. A tract of poor devil-stricken alkali flat, far away on the northeasterly side towards Bennett Hill, comfortless, treeless and bleak, was allowed by the Wilsons as an addition and forty or fifty families built homes there. But the Wilsons would not sell any of the rich lands abutting directly on the attractive portions of the main village street or the west or south. People of means and taste who wanted to live near the college, appealed in vain to the Wilsons. The Wilsons, though owning so many hundred acres, would not yield a few acres or even one foot for town lots; and these persons of refinement, discouraged, unwilling to build homes in the sterile and dreary alkali, gave up the hope of living in this little college town and went elsewhere. It is likely that anyone reading this spirited, indeed at times almost brilliant narrative of Luzena Wilson would infer the Wilsons were progressive and public-spirited. They were not—they cared only for the interests of the Wilsons, and for there [sic] interests narrowly.

The query stirs in my mind how Francis Farquhar became associated with the Luzena Wilson narrative and wrote the preface. Gay and festive in my temperament, I hazard the guess that it was because he knew utterly nothing about the Wilsons and acquired no knowledge save what as a literateur [sic] dealing in an ardent and scholarly way with "Californiana" he dug out of books or old records. His preface is very very happy. At the end he puts in that delightful little touch which in effect intimates they, the Wilsons, lived happily ever after. Unfortunately, for the story-book part of it, this implication is not in accordance with the factual record. Notice that Luzena always says "my" not "our." Luzena, Forty-niner, was a determined and strong-minded personage—a woman of the real pioneer type. But even so her husband, Mason Wilson, became wearied. He could stand Luzena no longer and he went away from Vaca Valley. He did not tell Luzena he was going nor anyone—he just got up and left, and put as much distance between himself and Luzena as he well could. He settled in Texas and from the first he prospered. He prospered so much that he sent soon for his name-sake son, Mason Wilson, who went and joined his father in Texas and stayed there. None of these matters nor many many others are mentioned by Luzena Wilson. It would be interesting to have her ideas on these and on kindred subjects. We may be sure her thoughts would have been expressive and forceful, although the telling diction and polished sentences would have been no other than those of her daughter Corrhena [sic], alumna of Mills College, because Mrs. Wilson, with all her many virtues, was still an uneducated and rugged pioneer.

So there are several reasons why, happily, Francis Farquhar wrote that preface. A romantic story-book tale needs a romantic preface, and Francis Farquhar perhaps did the job a lot better than he would if he known [sic] the Wilsons as some others knew them.

The Wilson children were smart children. Corrhena you have an idea of. Tom Wilson got, when a lad, a Congressional appointment to Annapolis. Whether he stayed for the full course I do not know, but he came to church in Vacaville in his naval uniform. He never accepted a commission. Many years ago, after he had become a mature man, I used to see him contentedly loafing in care-free indolence in the great easy chairs of the Bohemian Club.

I notice you spell it Ulattis Creek. On the earliest maps it is spelled Ulatis Creek. The student paper in the old-time college was called "The Ulatis." The first public school at Vacaville was the Ulatis Grammar School. There was later a men's club, The Ulatis Club. It is Ulatis Creek on the United States topographic maps. I imagine you got your spelling from some anthropologist. The first writer in literature to mention this Indian tribe was, so far as I know, Adelbert von Chamisso, who in 1816 speaks of the Ululatos, and of a few members of the tribe that had come to Mission Delores.

With many happy remembrances and best wishes

Faithfully yours,

Willis L. Jepson

BIBLIOGRAPHY

BOOKS

Anderson, Alvin L., Ph D., Stanley and Allied Families: *Descendants of the Quaker Stanley Families of Colonial Virginia,* Vols. 1 and 2, Gateway Press, Baltimore, 1996.

Bacon, Margaret H., *The Quiet Rebels,* Basic Books, New York and London, 1969.

Brown, Herrick Crosby, *Herrick Genealogy,* Pacific Rotaprinting Co., Oakland, 1950.

Cloud, Roy W., *Education in California: Leaders, Organizations, and Accomplishments of the First Hundred Years,* Stanford University Press, Stanford, California, 1952.

Comstock, David Allan, *Gold Diggers and Camp Followers,* Comstock Bonanza Press, Grass Valley, 1982.

Greene, Clay M., *The Annals of the Bohemian Club: From the Year 1895 to 1906 Inclusive,* Bohemian Club, San Francisco, 1930.

Guinn, Professor J. M., A.M., *History of the State of California and Biographical Record of the Sacramento Valley,* Chapman Publishing Co., Chicago, 1906.

Guinn, Professor J.M., Ph.D., *History of the State of California and Biographical Record of the Coast Counties,* Chapman Publishing Co., Chicago, 1904.

Healey, John, ed., *Editors West:* California Press Association Newspaper Hall of Fame, California Polytechnic State University, 1978.

Hedley, George, *Aurelia Reinhardt: Portrait of a Whole Woman,* Mills College, Oakland, 1961.

Hilty, Hiram H., *New Garden Friends Meeting: The Christian People Called Quakers,* North Carolina Friends Historical Society, North Carolina Yearly Meeting, New Garden Meeting, 1983.

Hilty, Hiram H., *By Land and Sea: Quakers Confront Slavery and Its Aftermath in North Carolina,* Friends Historical Society, Greensboro, North Carolina, 1993.

Hinshaw, Seth, *The Carolina Quaker Experience 1665–1985,* North Carolina Friends Historical Society, North Carolina Yearly Meeting, 1984.

Hinshaw, William Wade, *Encyclopedia of Quaker Genealogy,* Vol. 1. Reprint by Genealogical Publishing Co., Baltimore, 1969–1973.

History of Napa and Lake Counties, California, Slocum, Bowen & Co., San Francisco, 1881. Reprint by Valley Publishers, Fresno, California, 1974.

Holden, William M., *Sacramento: Excursions into its History and Natural World,* Two Rivers Publishing Co., Fair Oaks, California, 1987.

Hope Ranch, A. D. Shepard, Pacific Improvement Company, San Francisco, c. 1908.

Johnson, J. Edward, *History of the Supreme Court Justices of California,* Bender–Moss Co., San Francisco, 1963.

Keep, Rosalind A., *Fourscore and Ten Years: A History of Mills College,* Eucalyptus Press, Oakland, 1947.

Kibbey, Mead J., *Horace Culver's Sacramento City Directory for the year 1851,* California State Library Foundation, Sacramento, 2000.

Larkey, Joann Leach, *Winters: A Heritage of Agriculture, a Harmony of Purpose,* Yolo County Historical Society, Woodland, California, 1991.

Levy, Jo Ann, *They Saw the Elephant,* University of Oklahoma Press, Norman, 1992.

Limbaugh, Ronald H. and Walter A. Payne, *Vacaville: The Heritage of a California Community,* Vacaville City Council, Vacaville, 1978.

Lord, Israel Shipman Pelton, *At the Extremity of Civilization: An Illinois Physician's Journey to California in 1849,* McFarland & Co., Jefferson, North Carolina, 1995.

Lyons, Louis S. and Josephine Wilson, eds., *Who's Who among the Women of California,* Security Publishing Co., San Francisco, 1922.

Marryat, Frank, *Mountains and Molehills: or, Recollections of a Burnt Journal,* Harper & Brothers, New York, 1855. Reprint by J. B. Lippincott, Philadelphia and New York, 1962.

Massett, Stephen C., *Drifting About: or, What Jeems Pipes of Pipesville Saw—and Did,* Carleton, Publisher, New York, 1863.

McKenney's County Directory 1884–1885, L. M. McKenney & Co., San Francisco, 1883.

Memorial and Biographical History of McLennan, Falls, Bell and Coryell Counties, Texas, Lewis Publishing Co., Chicago, 1893.

Morse, John F., *The First History of Sacramento City written in 1853 by John Frederick Morse, M.D., with a historical note on the life of Dr. Morse,* by Caroline Wenzel. Reprint by Sacramento Book Collectors Club, Sacramento, 1945.

Pleasants, William J., *Twice Across the Plains: 1849 & 1856,* W.N. Brunt, San Francisco, 1906. Reprint by Ye Galleon Press, Fairfield, Washington, 1981.

Powell, William S., *North Carolina Through Four Centuries,* The University of North Carolina Press, Chapel Hill, 1989.

Rasmussen, Louis J., *California Wagon Train Lists,* Vol. 1, San Francisco Historic Records, Colma, 1994.

Royce, Sarah, *A Frontier Lady: Recollections of the Gold Rush and Early California,* Yale University Press, New Haven, 1932. Reprint by University of Nebraska Press, 1977.

Russell, William O., ed., *History of Yolo County, California: Its Resources and its People,* Woodland, California, 1940.

San Francisco City Directory, 1868–1934.

Sargent, Aaron Augustus, *1848–1851: 150 Years Ago,* reprinted from an account published in 1856, "A Sketch of Nevada County," arranged, illustrated and annotated by David Allan Comstock, *Nevada County Sesquicentennial,* 1998.

Sawyers, Sherry, *Mason County, Kentucky Marriage Bonds and Permissive Notes,* Vol. 1, Sherry Sawyers, Hamilton, Ohio, 1999.

Simpson, Anna Pratt, *Problems Women Solved: Being the Story of the Panama–Pacific International Exposition,* The Woman's Board, San Francisco, 1915.

Stewart, George R., *The California Trail: An Epic with Many Heroes,* McGraw–Hill Book Co., New York, 1962.

Takaki, Ronald T., *A Different Mirror: A History of Multicultural America,* Little, Brown and Co., Boston, Toronto and London, 1993.

Taylor, Bayard, *Eldorado: Adventures in the Path of Empire,* George P. Putnam, New York, 1850. Reprint by Heyday Books, Berkeley, California, 2000.

Third Annual Catalogue of Officers and Students of the Pacific Methodist College, Vacaville, 1863–1864 and 1864–1865, San Francisco.

Thissell, G. W., *Crossing the Plains in '49,* Oakland, California, 1903.

Thompson and West, *History of Sacramento County, California,* Oakland, 1880.

United States, Naval War Records Office, *Official Records of the Union and Confederate Navies in the War of the Rebellion,* Washington, 1921.

Vital Records of Windsor, Massachusetts to the year 1850, New England Historic Genealogical Society, Boston, 1917.

Vivian, Imogene Holbrook, *A Biographical Sketch of the life of Charles Algernon Sidney Vivian,* Whitaker and Ray Co., San Francisco, 1903.

Weeks, Stephen B., *Southern Quakers and Slavery,* Johns Hopkins Press, 1896. Reprint by Bergman Publishers, New York, 1968.

Wells, Harry L., J. Albert Wilson, H. G. Rice and Allen Freeman, *History of Nevada County, California,* Thompson and West, Oakland, 1880.

Wilson, Luzena Stanley, *Luzena Stanley Wilson: '49er: Memories Recalled Years Later for Her Daughter, Correnah Wilson Wright,* Eucalyptus Press, Mills College, Oakland,.

Wood, Alley and Company, *The History of Solano County,* San Francisco, 1879. Reprint by James Stevenson Publisher, Fairfield, California, 1994.

Young, Wood, *Vaca–Peña Los Putos Rancho and the Peña Adobe,* Wheeler Printing and Publishing Co., Vallejo, 1965.

NEWSPAPERS AND PERIODICALS

Alta California, 1850, 1851, 1858, 1860, 1877

Argonaut, 1881.

Bancroft's Guide for Travelers by Railway, Stage and Steam Navigation in the Pacific States, 1869.

Golden Notes, Sacramento Historical Society, 1980, 1986

Lakeport Bee Democrat, 1880, 1882

Placer Times, 1849, 1850

Red Bluff Weekly News, 1914

Sacramento Transcript, 1850, 1851

San Francisco Call, 1868, 1886, 1889, 1902, 1905, 1934, 1964

San Francisco Chronicle, 1910, 1926, 1934

San Francisco Examiner, 1917, 1921, 1924, 1926, 1934

Solano County Herald, 1857, 1867, 1868, 1869

Vacaville Reporter, 1883, 1884, 1901, 1903, 1904, 1905, 1906, 1907, 1948, 1974, 1981

Weekly Solano Herald, 1867, 1868, 1869

Weekly Solano Republican, 1872, 1873, 1874, 1877

Woodland Daily Democrat, 1899

Yolo Semi-Weekly Mail, 1896

UNPUBLISHED MATERIAL

Century Club of California, Seventeenth Annual Report, San Francisco.

Hall, Edwin G., letter, October 26, 1849, California State Library.

Harbison, Luther and Melissa, letters in Harbison Collection, Vacaville Museum.

Jepson, Willis Linn, letter, March 21, 1939, Jepson Herbarium, University of California, Berkeley.

Minutes of the New Garden Monthly Meeting, Friends Historical Collection, Guilford College, Greensboro, North Carolina.

LIBRARIES AND ARCHIVES

Andrew County, Missouri, Recorder of Deeds
Bancroft Library, University of California, Berkeley
California Genealogical Society
California State Department Records
California State Library
Central Texas Genealogical Society
Church of Jesus Christ of Latter Day Saints, Family History Center
Harvard Law School Library, Special Collections
Lake County Library
Lake County Museum
McLennan County, Texas, Recorded Deeds
Military and Pension Files
Mills College Alumnae Association
Mills College, Special Collections, F. W. Olin Library
National Archives and Records Administration
Nevada County History Branch Library
North Yorkshire County Council, Register Office, Harrogate, England
Sacramento Archives and Museum Collection Center
Sacramento Public Library, Sacramento Room
San Francisco County
    Assessor–Recorder Office
    Coroner's Office
    Court Probate Records
San Francisco Performing Arts Library
San Francisco Public Library, San Francisco History Center
Sisters of Notre Dame de Namur, California Province Archives, Belmont, California
Society of California Pioneers
Solano County Archives
    Court Records
    Deeds and Assessment Records
Solano County Genealogical Society Library
Solano County Library, Vacaville and Fairfield Branches
Solano County Office of Education
Solano Heritage Council
United States Bureau of Land Management, Government Land Office Records, Missouri
United States Census Bureau
Vacaville Museum
Waco Public Library
Wells Fargo History Museum
William W. Jeffries Memorial Archives, United States Naval Academy
Yolo County History Museum

ARTICLES AND PAPERS

Carothers, Neil, "Isaac Crocker: An Adventure in Genealogy," *Connecticut Historical Society Bulletin,* Vol. 24, No. 1, Hartford, 1959.

Crystal, Helen Carmody, "The Beginnings of Vacaville," Master's thesis, History Department, University of California, Berkeley, 1923.

Dickie, Alexander J., "Early San Francisco Shipping: Early Steamers," *Pacific Marine Review,* San Francisco, April, 1948.

Miller, Jean Marie, "Pacific Methodist College at Vacaville," term paper, Sacramento State College, December 30, 1962, Vacaville Museum files.

Nagel, Charles E., "A Fight for Survival: Floods, Riots, and Disease in Sacramento 1850," Master's thesis, Sacramento City College, 1965.

Royce, Josiah, "The Squatter Riot of '50 in Sacramento: Its Causes and Significance," *The Overland Monthly,* Vol. 6, Second Series, September, 1885, No. 33.

Stephens, Meredith, "The Vaca Valley and Clear Lake Railroad," term paper, March 3, 1971, Vacaville Museum files.

Wilson, Luzena Stanley Wilson, "A Woman's Reminiscences of Early Days," *Argonaut,* February–April, 1881.

PERSONAL COMMUNICATIONS

Anderson, Dr. Alvin, e-mail, July 22, 2001 and August 10, 2001.

Buff, Matthew, Bohemian Club, letter, January 10, 2001.

Egan, SND, Sister Janet Marie, letter, May 17, 2001.

Gibbons, Mrs. Henry, Century Club of California, interview, June 8, 2000.

Jones, Cora Lee, letter, February 7, 2001.

Lampen, Betty, The Metropolitan Club, letter, April 28, 2001.

Larkey, Joann L., interview, May 10, 2001.

Morton, Anne and Tom, interview, April, 2001.

Pangburn, Frank, e-mail, May 13, 2002.

Sirkin, Jeff, Harvard Law School Alumni Center, e-mail, April 21, 2000.

Weston, Nancy Perrin, The National Society of the Colonial Dames of America in California, letter, March 27, 2001.

INDEX